The Wit of Women

by Kate Sanborn

INTRODUCTION.

It is refreshing to find an unworked field all ready for harvesting.

While the wit of men, as a subject for admiration and discussion, is now threadbare, the wit of women has been almost utterly ignored and unrecognized.

With the joy and honest pride of a discoverer, I present the results of a summer's gleaning.

And I feel a cheerful and Colonel Sellers-y confidence in the success of the book, for every woman will want to own it, as a matter of pride and interest, and many men will buy it just to see what women think they can do in this line. In fact, I expect a call for a second volume!

KATE SANBORN. HANOVER, N.H., August, 1885.

My thanks are due to so many publishers, magazine editors, and personal friends for material for this book, that a formal note of acknowledgment seems meagre and unsatisfactory. Proper credit, however, has been given all through the volume, and with special indebtedness to Messrs. Harper & Brothers and Charles Scribner's Sons of New York, and Houghton, Mifflin & Co. of Boston. I add sincere gratitude to all who have so generously contributed whatever was requested.

CONTENTS.

GOOD-NATURED SATIRE

CHAPTER X.

TO G.W.B. In Grateful Memory.

"There was in her soul a sense of delicacy mingled with that rarest of qualities in woman--a sense of humor," writes Richard Grant White in "The Fate of Mansfield Humphreys." I have noticed that when a novelist sets out to portray an uncommonly fine type of heroine, he invariably adds to her other intellectual and moral graces the above-mentioned "rarest of qualities." I may be over-sanguine, but I anticipate that some sagacious genius will discover that woman as well as man has been endowed with this excellent gift from the gods, and that the gift pertains to the large, generous, sympathetic nature, quite irrespective of the individual's sex. In any case, having heard so repeatedly that woman has no sense of humor, it would be refreshing to have a contrariety of opinion on that subject.--THE CRITIC.

PROEM.[A]

We are coming to the rescue, Just a hundred strong; With fun and pun and epigram, And laughter, wit, and song;

With badinage and repartee, And humor quaint or bold, And stories that are stories, Not several eons old;

With parody and nondescript, Burlesque and satire keen, And irony and playful jest, So that it may be seen

That women are not quite so dull: We come--a merry throng; Yes, we're coming to the rescue, And just a hundred strong.

KATE SANBORN. [Footnote A: Not Poem!]

THE WIT OF WOMEN.

CHAPTER I.

THE MELANCHOLY TONE OF WOMEN'S POETRY--PUNS, GOOD AND BAD--
EPIGRAMS AND LACONICS--CYNICISM OF FRENCH WOMEN--SENTENCES
CRISP AND SPARKLING.

To begin a deliberate search for wit seems almost like trying to be witty: a
task quite certain to brush the bloom from even the most fruitful results. But
the statement of Richard Grant White, that humor is the "rarest of qualities in
woman," roused such a host of brilliant recollections that it was a temptation
to try to materialize the ghosts that were haunting me; to lay forever the
suspicion that they did not exist. Two articles by Alice Wellington Rollins in
the Critic, on "Woman's Sense of Humor" and "The Humor of Women,"
convinced me that the deliberate task might not be impossible to carry out,
although I felt, as she did, that the humor and wit of women are difficult to
analyze, and select examples, precisely because they possess in the highest
degree that almost essential quality of wit, the unpremeditated glow which
exists only with the occasion that calls it forth. Even from the humor of
women found in books it is hard to quote--not because there is so little, but
because there is so much.

The encouragement to attempt this novel enterprise of proving ("by their
fruits ye shall know them") that women are not deficient in either wit or
humor has not been great. Wise librarians have, with a smile, regretted the
paucity of proper material; literary men have predicted rather a thin volume;
in short, the general opinion of men is condensed in the sly question of a
peddler who comes to our door, summer and winter, his stock varying with
the season: sage-cheese and home-made socks, suspenders and cheap note-
paper, early-rose potatoes and the solid pearmain. This shrewd old fellow
remarked roguishly "You're gittin' up a book, I see, 'baout women's wit.
'Twon't be no great of an undertakin', will it?" The outlook at first was
certainly discouraging. In Parton's "Collection of Humorous Poetry" there was
not one woman's name, nor in Dodd's large volume of epigrams of all ages,
nor in any of the humorous departments of volumes of selected poetry.

Griswold's "Female Poets of America" was next examined. The general air of
gloom--hopeless gloom--was depressing. Such mawkish sentimentality and

despair; such inane and mortifying confessions; such longings for a lover to come; such sighings over a lover departed; such cravings for "only"--"only" a grave in some dark, dank solitude. As Mrs. Dodge puts it, "Pegasus generally feels inclined to pace toward a graveyard the moment he feels a side-saddle on his back."

The subjects of their lucubrations suggest Lady Montagu's famous speech: "There was only one reason she was glad she was a woman: she should never have to marry one."

From the "Female Poets" I copy this "Song," representing the average woman's versifying as regards buoyancy and an optimistic view of this "Wale of Tears":

"Ask not from me the sportive jest, The mirthful jibe, the gay reflection; These social baubles fly the breast That owns the sway of pale Dejection.

"Ask not from me the changing smile, Hope's sunny glow, Joy's glittering token; It cannot now my griefs beguile-- My soul is dark, my heart is broken!

"Wit cannot cheat my heart of woe, Flattery wakes no exultation; And Fancy's flash but serves to show The darkness of my desolation!

"By me no more in masking guise Shall thoughtless repartee be spoken; My mind a hopeless ruin lies-- My soul is dark, my heart is broken!"

In recalling the witty women of the world, I must surely go back, familiar as is the story, to the Grecian dame who, when given some choice old wine in a tiny glass by her miserly host, who boasted of the years since it had been bottled, inquired, "Isn't it very small of its age?"

This ancient story is too much in the style of the male story-monger--you all know him--who repeats with undiminished gusto for the forty-ninth time a story that was tottering in senile imbecility when Methuselah was teething, and is now in a sad condition of anecdotage.

It is affirmed that "women seldom repeat an anecdote." That is well, and no proof of their lack of wit. The discipline of life would be largely increased if they did insist on being "reminded" constantly of anecdotes as familiar as the hand-organ repertoire of "Captain Jinks" and "Beautiful Spring." Their sense of humor is too keen to allow them to aid these aged wanderers in their endless migrations. It is sufficiently trying to their sense of the ludicrous to be obliged to listen with an admiring, rapt expression to some anecdote heard in childhood, and restrain the laugh until the oft-repeated crisis has been duly reached. Still, I know several women who, as brilliant raconteurs, have fully equalled the efforts of celebrated after-dinner wits.

It is also affirmed that "women cannot make a pun," which, if true, would be greatly to their honor. But, alas! their puns are almost as frequent and quite as execrable as are ever perpetrated. It was Queen Elizabeth who said: "Though ye be burly, my Lord Burleigh, ye make less stir than my Lord Leicester."

Lady Morgan, the Irish novelist, witty and captivating, who wrote "Kate Kearney" and the "Wild Irish Girl," made several good puns. Some one, speaking of the laxity of a certain bishop in regard to Lenten fasting, said: "I believe he would eat a horse on Ash Wednesday." "And very proper diet," said her ladyship, "if it were a fast horse."

Her special enemy, Croker, had declared that Wellington's success at Waterloo was only a fortunate accident, and intimated that he could have done better himself, under similar circumstances. "Oh, yes," exclaimed her ladyship, "he had his secret for winning the battle. He had only to put his notes on Boswell's Johnson in front of the British lines, and all the Bonapartes that ever existed could never get through them!"

"Grace Greenwood" has probably made more puns in print than any other woman, and her conversation is full of them. It was Grace Greenwood who, at a tea-drinking at the Woman's Club in Boston, was begged to tell one more story, but excused herself in this way: "No, I cannot get more than one story high on a cup of tea!"

You see puns are allowed at that rarely intellectual assemblage--indeed, they are sometimes very bad; as when the question was brought up whether better speeches could be made after simple tea and toast, or under the influence of champagne and oysters. Miss Mary Wadsworth replied that it would depend entirely upon whether the oysters were cooked or raw; and seeing all look blank, she explained: "Because, if raw, we should be sure to have a raw-oyster-ing time."

Louisa Alcott's puns deserve "honorable mention." I will quote one. "Query-- If steamers are named the Asia, the Russia, and the Scotia, why not call one the Nausea?"

At a Chicago dinner-party a physician received a menu card with the device of a mushroom, and showing it to the lady next him, said: "I hope nothing invidious is intended." "Oh, no," was the answer, "it only alludes to the fact that you spring up in the night."

A gentleman, noticeable on the porch of the sanctuary as the pretty girls came in on Sabbath mornings, but not regarded as a devout attendant on the services within, declared that he was one of the "pillars of the church!" "Pillar-sham, I am inclined to think," was the retort of a lady friend.

To a lady who, in reply to a gentleman's assertion that women sometimes made a good pun, but required time to think about it, had said that she could make a pun as quickly as any man, the gentleman threw down this challenge: "Make a pun, then, on horse-shoe." "If you talk until you're horse-shoe can't convince me," was the instant answer.

* * * * *

The best punning poem from a woman's pen was written by Miss Caroline B. Le Row, of Brooklyn, N.Y., a teacher of elocution, and the writer of many charming stories and verses. It was suggested by a study in butter of "The Dreaming Iolanthe," moulded by Caroline S. Brooks on a kitchen-table, and exhibited at the Centennial in Philadelphia. I do not remember any other poem in the language that rings so many changes on a single word. It was published first in Baldwin's Monthly, but ran the rounds of the papers all over the country.

I.

"One of the Centennial buildings Shows us many a wondrous thing Which the women of our country From their homes were proud to bring. In a little corner, guarded By Policeman Twenty-eight, Stands a crowd, all eyes and elbows, Seeing butter butter-plate

II.

"'Tis not 'butter faded flower' That the people throng to see, Butter crowd comes every hour, Nothing butter crowd we see. Butter little pushing brings us Where we find, to our surprise, That within the crowded corner Butter dreaming woman lies.

III.

"Though she lies, she don't deceive us, As it might at first be thought; This fair maid is made of butter, On a kitchen-table wrought. Nothing butter butter-paddle, Sticks and straws were used to bring Out of just nine pounds of butter Butter fascinating thing.

IV.

"Butter maid or made of butter, She is butter wonder rare; Butter sweet eyes closed in slumber, Butter soft and yellow hair, Were the work of butter woman Just two thousand miles away; Butter fortune's in the features That she made in butter stay.

V.

"Maid of all work, maid of honor, Whatsoever she may be, She is butter wondrous worker, As the crowd can plainly see. And 'tis butter woman shows us What with butter can be done, Nothing butter hands producing Something new beneath the sun.

VI.

"Butter line we add in closing, Which none butter could refuse: May her work be butter pleasure, Nothing butter butter use; May she never need for butter, Though she'll often knead for bread, And may every churning bring her Butter blessing on her head."

* * * * *

The second and last example is much more common in its form, but is just as good as most of the verses of this style in Parton's "Humorous Poetry." I don't pretend that it is remarkable, but it is equally worthy of presentation with many efforts of this sort from men with a reputation for wit.

THE VEGETABLE GIRL.

BY MAY TAYLOR.

Behind a market-stall installed, I mark it every day, Stands at her stand the fairest girl I've met within the bay; Her two lips are of cherry red, Her hands a pretty pair, With such a charming turn-up nose, And lovely reddish hair.

'Tis there she stands from morn till night, Her customers to please, And to appease their appetite She sells them beans and peas. Attracted by the glances from The apple of her eye, And by her Chili apples, too, Each passer-by will buy.

She stands upon her little feet Throughout the livelong day, And sells her celery and things-- A big feat, by the way. She changes off her stock for change, Attending to each call; And when she has but one beet left, She says, "Now, that beats all."

* * * * *

As to puns in conversation, my only fear is that they are too generally indulged in. Only one of this sort can be allowed, and that from the highest lady in the land, who is distinguished for culture and good sense, as well as wit. A friend said to her as she was leaving Buffalo for Washington: "I hope you will hail from Buffalo."

"Oh, I see you expect me to hail from Buffalo and reign in Washington," said the quick-witted sister of our President.

In epigrams there is little to offer. But as it is stated that "women cannot achieve a well-rounded epigram," a few specimens must be produced.

Jane Austen has left two on record. The first was suggested by reading in a newspaper the marriage of a Mr. Gell to Miss Gill, of Eastborne.

"At Eastborne, Mr. Gell, from being perfectly well, Became dreadfully ill for love of Miss Gill; So he said, with some sighs, 'I'm the slave of your iis; Oh, restore, if you please, by accepting my ees.'"

The second is on the marriage of a middle-aged flirt with a Mr. Wake, whom gossips averred she would have scorned in her prime.

"Maria, good-humored and handsome and tall, For a husband was at her last stake; And having in vain danced at many a ball, Is now happy to jump at a Wake."

It was Lady Townsend who said that the human race was divided into men, women, and Herveys. This epigram has been borrowed in our day, substituting for Herveys the Beecher family.

When some one said of a lady she must be in spirits, for she lives with Mr. Walpole, "Yes," replied Lady Townsend, "spirits of hartshorn."

Walpole, caustic and critical, regarded this lady as undeniably witty.

It was Hannah More who said: "There are but two bad things in this world-- sin and bile."

Miss Thackeray quotes several epigrammatic definitions from her friend Miss Evans, as:

"A privileged person: one who is so much a savage when thwarted that civilized persons avoid thwarting him."

"A musical woman: one who has strength enough to make much noise and obtuseness enough not to mind it."

"Ouida" has given us some excellent examples of epigram, as:

"A pipe is a pocket philosopher, a truer one than Socrates, for it never asks questions. Socrates must have been very tiresome, when one thinks of it."

"Dinna ye meddle, Tam; it's niver no good a threshin' other folks' corn; ye allays gits the flail agin' i' yer own eye somehow."

"Epigrams are the salts of life; but they wither up the grasses of foolishness, and naturally the grasses hate to be sprinkled therewith."

"A man never is so honest as when he speaks well of himself. Men are always optimists when they look inward, and pessimists when they look round them."

"Nothing is so pleasant as to display your worldly wisdom in epigram and dissertation, but it is a trifle tedious to hear another person display theirs."

"When you talk yourself you think how witty, how original, how acute you are; but when another does so, you are very apt to think only, 'What a crib from Rochefoucauld!'"

"Boredom is the ill-natured pebble that always will get in the golden slipper of the pilgrim of pleasure."

"It makes all the difference in life whether hope is left or--left out!"

"A frog that dwelt in a ditch spat at a worm that bore a lamp.

"'Why do you do that?' said the glow-worm.

"'Why do you shine?' said the frog."

"Calumny is the homage of our contemporaries, as some South Sea Islanders spit on those they honor."

"Hived bees get sugar because they will give back honey. All existence is a series of equivalents."

"'Men are always like Horace,' said the Princess. 'They admire rural life, but they remain, for all that, with Augustus.'"

"If the Venus de Medici could be animated into life, women would only remark that her waist was large."

* * * * *

The brilliant Frenchwomen whose very names seem to sparkle as we write them, yet of whose wit so little has been preserved, had an especial facility for condensed cynicism.

Think of Madame du Deffand, sceptical, sarcastic; feared and hated even in her blind old age for her scathing criticisms. When the celebrated work of Helvetius appeared he was blamed in her presence for having made selfishness the great motive of human action.

"Bah!" said she, "he has only revealed every one's secret."

And listen to this trio of laconics, with their saddening knowledge of human frailty and their bitter Voltaireish flavor:

We shall all be perfectly virtuous when there is no longer any flesh on our bones.--Marguerite de Valois.

We like to know the weakness of eminent persons; it consoles us for our inferiority.--Mme. de Lambert.

Women give themselves to God when the devil wants nothing more to do with them.--Sophie Arnould.

Madame de Savigne's letters present detached thoughts worthy of Rochefoucauld without his cynicism. She writes: "One loves so much to talk of one's self that one never tires of a tete-tete with a lover for years. That is the reason that a devotee likes to be with her confessor. It is for the pleasure of talking of one's self--even though speaking evil." And she remarks to a lady who amused her friends by always going into mourning for some prince, or duke, or member of some royal family, and who at last appeared in bright colors, "Madame, I congratulate myself on the health of Europe."

I find, too, many fine aphorisms from "Carmen Sylva" (Queen of Roumania):

In the recently published sketch of Madame Mohl there are several sentences which show trenchant wit, as: "Nations squint in looking at one another; we must discount what Germany and France say of each other."

Several Englishwomen can be recalled who were noted for their epigrammatic wit: as Harriet, Lady Ashburton. On some one saying that liars generally speak good-naturedly of others, she replied: "Why, if you don't speak a word of truth, it is not so difficult to speak well of your neighbor."

"Don't speak so hardly of ----," some one said to her; "he lives on your good graces."

"That accounts," she answered, "for his being so thin."

Again: "I don't mind the canvas of a man's mind being good, if only it is completely hidden by the worsted and floss."

Or: "She never speaks to any one, which is, of course, a great advantage to any one."

Mrs. Carlyle was an epigram herself--small, sweet, yet possessing a sting-- and her letters give us many sharp and original sayings.

She speaks in one place of "Mrs. ----, an insupportable bore; her neck and arms were as naked as if she had never eaten of the tree of the knowledge of good and evil."

And what a comical phrase is hers when she writes to her "Dearest"--"I take time by the pig-tail and write at night, after post-hours"--that growling, surly "dearest," of whom she said, "The amount of bile that he brings home is awfully grand."

For a veritable epigram from an American woman's pen we must rely on Hannah F. Gould, who wrote many verses that were rather graceful and arch than witty. But her epitaph on her friend, the active and aggressive Caleb Cushing, is as good as any made by Saxe.

"Lay aside, all ye dead, For in the next bed Reposes the body of Cushing; He has crowded his way Through the world, they say, And even though dead will be pushing."

Such a hit from a bright woman is refreshing.

Our literary foremothers seemed to prefer to be pedantic, didactic, and tedious on the printed page.

Catharine Sedgwick dealt somewhat in epigram, as when she says: "He was not one of those convenient single people who are used, as we use straw and cotton in packing, to fill up vacant places."

Eliza Leslie (famed for her cook-books and her satiric sketches), when speaking of people silent from stupidity, supposed kindly to be full of reserved power, says: "We cannot help thinking that when a head is full of ideas some of them must involuntarily ooze out."

And is not this epigrammatic advice? "Avoid giving invitations to bores--they will come without."

Some of our later literary women prefer the epigrammatic form in sentences, crisp and laconic; short sayings full of pith, of which I have made a collection.

Gail Hamilton's books fairly bristle with epigrams in condensed style, and Kate Field has many a good thought in this shape, as: "Judge no one by his relations, whatever criticism you pass upon his companions. Relations, like features, are thrust upon us; companions, like clothes, are more or less our own selection."

Miss Jewett's style is less epigrammatic, but just as full of humor. Speaking of a person who was always complaining, she says: "Nothing ever suits her. She ain't had no more troubles to bear than the rest of us; but you never see her that she didn't have a chapter to lay before ye. I've got 's much feelin' as the next one, but when folks drives in their spiggits and wants to draw a bucketful o' compassion every day right straight along, there does come times when it seems as if the bar'l was getting low."

"The captain, whose eyes were not much better than his ears, always refused to go forth after nightfall without his lantern. The old couple steered slowly down the uneven sidewalk toward their cousin's house. The captain walked with a solemn, rolling gait, learned in his many long years at sea, and his wife, who was also short and stout, had caught the habit from him. If they kept step all went well; but on this occasion, as sometimes happened, they did not take the first step out into the world together, so they swayed apart, and then bumped against each other as they went along. To see the lantern coming through the mist you might have thought it the light of a small craft at sea in heavy weather."

"Deaf people hear more things that are worth listening to than people with better ears; one likes to have something worth telling in talking to a person who misses most of the world's talk."

"Emory Ann," a creation of Mrs. Whitney's, often spoke in epigrams, as: "Good looks are a snare; especially to them that haven't got 'em." While Mrs. Walker's creed, "I believe in the total depravity of inanimate things," is more than an epigram--it is an inspiration.

Charlotte Fiske Bates, who compiled the "Cambridge Book of Poetry," and has given us a charming volume of her own verses, which no one runs any "Risk" in buying, in spite of the title of the book, has done a good deal in this direction, and is fond of giving an epigrammatic turn to a bright thought, as in the following couplet:

"Would you sketch in two words a coquette and deceiver? Name two Irish geniuses, Lover and Lever!"

She also succeeds with the quatrain:

ON BEING CALLED A GOOSE.

A signal name is this, upon my word! Great Juno's geese saved Rome her citadel. Another drowsy Manlius may be stirred And the State saved, if I but cackle well.

* * * * *

I recall a charming jeu d'esprit from Mrs. Barrows, the beloved "Aunt Fanny," who writes equally well for children and grown folks, and whose big heart ranges from earnest philanthropy to the perpetration of exquisite nonsense.

It is but a trifle, sent with a couple of peanut-owls to a niece of Bryant's. The aged poet was greatly amused.

"When great Minerva chose the Owl, That bird of solemn phiz, That truly awful-looking fowl, To represent her wis- Dom, little recked the goddess of The time when she would howl To see a Peanut set on end, And called-- Minerva's Owl."

* * * * *

Miss Phelps has given us some sentences which convey an epigram in a keen and delicate fashion, as:

"All forms of self-pity, like Prussian blue, should be sparingly used."

"As a rule, a man can't cultivate his mustache and his talents impartially."

"As happy as a kind-hearted old lady with a funeral to go to."

"No men are so fussy about what they eat as those who think their brains the biggest part of them."

"The professor's sister, a homeless widow, of excellent Vermont intentions and high ideals in cup-cake."

And this longer extract has the same characteristics:

"You know how it is with people, Avis; some take to zoology, and some take to religion. That's the way it is with places. It may be the Lancers, and it may be prayer-meetings. Once I went to see my grandmother in the country, and everybody had a candy-pull; there were twenty-five candy-pulls and taffy-bakes in that town that winter. John Rose says, in the Connecticut Valley, where he came from, it was missionary barrels; and I heard of a place where it was cold coffee. In Harmouth it's improving your mind. And so," added Coy, "we run to reading-clubs, and we all go fierce, winter after winter, to see who'll get the 'severest.' There's a set outside of the faculty that descends to charades and music and inconceivably low intellectual depths; and some of our girls sneak off and get in there once in a while, like the little girl that wanted to go from heaven to hell to play Saturday afternoons, just as you and I used to do, Avis, when we dared. But I find I've got too old for that," said Coy, sadly. "When you're fairly past the college-boys, and as far along as the law students--"

"Or the theologues?" interposed Avis.

"Yes, or the theologues, or even the medical department; then there positively is nothing for it but to improve your mind."

Listen to Lavinia, one of Mrs. Rose Terry Cooke's sensible Yankee women:

"Land! if you want to know folks, just hire out to 'em. They take their wigs off afore the help, so to speak, seemingly."

"Marryin' a man ain't like settin' alongside of him nights and hearin' him talk pretty; that's the fust prayer. There's lots an' lots o' meetin' after that!"

And what an amount of sense, as well as wit, in Sam Lawson's sayings in "Old Town Folks." As this book is not to be as large as Worcester's Unabridged Dictionary, I can only give room to one.

"We don't none of us like to have our sins set in order afore us. There was David, now, he was crank as could be when he thought Nathan was a talkin' about other people's sins. Says David: 'The man that did that shall surely die.' But come to set it home and say, 'Thou art the man!' David caved right in. 'Lordy massy, bless your soul and body, Nathan!' says he, 'I don't want to die.'"

And Mrs. A.D.T. Whitney must not be forgotten. "As Emory Ann said once about thoughts: 'You can't hinder 'em any more than you can the birds that fly in the air; but you needn't let 'em light and make a nest in your hair.'"

And what a capital hit on the hypocritical apologies of conceited housekeepers is this bit from Mrs. Whicher ("Widow Bedott"): "A person that didn't know how wimmin always go on at such a place would a thought that Miss Gipson had tried to have everything the miserablest she possibly could, and that the rest on 'em never had anything to hum but what was miserabler yet."

And Marietta Holley, who has caused a tidal-wave of laughter by her "Josiah Allen's Wife" series, shall have her say.

"We, too, are posterity, though mebby we don't realize it as we ort to."

"She didn't seem to sense anything, only ruffles and such like. Her mind all seemed to be narrowed down and puckered up, just like trimmin'."

But I must have convinced the most sceptical of woman's wit in epigrammatic form, and will now return to an older generation, who claim a fair share of attention.

CHAPTER II.

HUMOR OF LITERARY ENGLISHWOMEN.

In reviewing the bon-mots of Stella, whom Swift pronounced the most witty woman he had ever known, it seems that we are improving. I will give but two of her sayings, which were so carefully preserved by her friend.

When she was extremely ill her physician said, "Madam, you are near the bottom of the hill, but we will endeavor to get you up again;" she answered: "Doctor, I fear I shall be out of breath before I get up to the top."

After she had been eating some sweet thing a little of it happened to stick on her lips. A gentleman told her of it, and offered to lick it off. She said: "No, sir, I thank you; I have a tongue of my own."

Compare these with the wit of George Eliot or the irony of Miss Phelps.

Some of Jane Taylor's stories and poems were formerly regarded as humorous; for instance, the "Discontented Pendulum" and the "Philosopher's Scales." They do not now raise the faintest smile.

Fanny Burney's novels were considered immensely humorous and diverting in their day. Burke complimented her on "her natural vein of humor," and another eminent critic speaks of "her sarcasm, drollery, and humor;" but it would be almost impossible to find a passage for quotation that would now satisfy on these points. Even Jane Austen's novels, which strangely retain their hold on the public taste, are tedious to those who dare to think for themselves and forget Macaulay's verdict.

Mrs. Barbauld, in her poem on "Washing Day," shows a capacity seldom exercised for seeing the humorous side of every-day miseries.

"Woe to the friend Whose evil stars have urged him forth to claim On such a day the hospitable rites! Looks, blank at best, and stinted courtesy Shall he receive. Vainly he feeds his hopes With dinner of roast chicken, savory pie, Or tart, or pudding; pudding he nor tart That day shall eat; nor, though the husband try Mending what can't be helped to kindle mirth From cheer deficient, shall his consort's brow Cheer up propitious; the unlucky guest In silence dines, and early slinks away."

But her style is too stiff and stately for every day.

There were many literary Englishwomen who had undoubted humor. Hannah More did get unendurably poky, narrow, and solemn in her last days, and not a little sanctimonious; and we naturally think of her as an aged spinster with black mitts, corkscrew curls, and a mob cap, always writing or presenting a tedious tract, forgetting her brilliant youth, when she was quite good enough, and lively, too. She was a perennial favorite in London, meeting all the notables; the special pet of Dr. Johnson, Davy Garrick, and Horace Walpole, who called her his "holy Hannah," but admired and honored her, corresponding with her through a long life. She was then full of spirit and humor and versatile talent. An extract from her sister's lively letter shows that Hannah could hold her own with the Ursa Major of literature:

"Tuesday evening we drank tea at Sir Joshua's with Dr. Johnson. Hannah is certainly a great favorite. She was placed next him, and they had the entire conversation to themselves. They were both in remarkably high spirits. It was certainly her lucky night. I never heard her say so many good things. The old genius was extremely jocular, and the young one very pleasant. You would have imagined we had been at some comedy had you heard our peals of laughter. They, indeed, tried which could pepper the highest, and it is not clear to me that the lexicographer was really the highest seasoner."

And how deliciously does she set out the absurdity then prevailing, and seen now in editions of Shakespeare and Chaucer, of writing books, the bulk of which consists of notes, with only a line or two at the top of each page of the original text.

It seems that a merry party at Dr. Kennicott's had each adopted the name of some animal. Dr. K. was the elephant; Mrs. K., dromedary; Miss Adams, antelope; and H. More, rhinoceros.

"HAMPTON, December 24, 1728.

"DEAR DROMY (a): Pray, send word if Ante (b) is come, and also how Ele (c) does, to your very affectionate RHYNEY" (d).

The following notes on the above epistle are by a commentator of the latter end of the nineteenth century. This epistle is all that is come down to us of this voluminous author, and is probably the only thing she ever wrote that was worth preserving, or which might reasonably expect to reach posterity. Her name is only presented to us in some beautiful hendecasyllables written by the best Latin poet of his time (Bishop Lowth):

Note (a).

"Dromy.--From the termination of this address it seems to have been written to a woman, though there is no internal evidence to support this hypothesis. The best critics are much puzzled about the orthography of this abbreviation. Wartonius and other skilful etymologists contend that it ought to be spelled drummy, being addressed to a lady who was probably fond of warlike instruments, and who had a singular predilection for a canon. Drummy, say they, was a tender diminutive of drum, as the best authors in their more familiar writings now begin to use gunny for gun. But Hardius, a contemporary critic, contends, with more probability, that it ought to be written Drome, from hippodrome; a learned leech and elegant bard of Bath having left it on record that this lady spent much of her time at the riding-school, being a very exquisite judge of horsemanship. Colmanus and Horatius Strawberryensis insist that it ought to be written Dromo, in reference to the Dromo Sorasius of the Latin dramatist."

Note (b).

"Ante.--Scaliger 2d says this name simply signifies the appellation of uncle's wife, and ought to be written Aunty. But here, again, are various readings. Philologists of yet greater name affirm that it was meant to designate pre-eminence, and therefore ought to be written ante, before, from the Latin, a language now pretty well forgotten, though the authors who wrote in it are still preserved in French translations. The younger Madame Dacier insists that this lady was against all men, and that it ought to be spelled anti; but this Kennicotus, a rabbi of the most recondite learning, with much critical wrath, vehemently contradicts, affirming it to have been impossible she could have been against mankind whom all mankind admired. He adds that ante is for antelope, and is emblematically used to express an elegant and slender animal, or that it is an elongation of ant, the emblem of virtuous citizenship."

And so she continues her comments to close of notes.

Mrs. Gaskell's "Cranford" is full of the most delicate but veritable humor, as her allusion to the genteel and cheerful poverty of the lady who, in giving a tea-party, "now sat in state, pretending not to know what cakes were sent up, though she knew, and we knew, and she knew that we knew; and we knew that she knew that we knew she had been busy all the morning making tea-bread and sponge-cakes."

The humor of Mary Russell Mitford, quiet and delectable, must not be forgotten. We will sympathize with her woes as she describes a visitation from

THE TALKING LADY.

"Ben Jonson has a play called The Silent Woman, who turns out, as might be expected, to be no woman at all--nothing, as Master Slender said, but 'a great lubberly boy,' thereby, as I apprehend, discourteously presuming that a silent woman is a nonentity. If the learned dramatist, thus happily prepared and predisposed, had happened to fall in with such a specimen of female loquacity as I have just parted with, he might, perhaps, have given us a pendant to his picture in the talking lady. Pity but he had! He would have done her justice, which I could not at any time, least of all now; I am too much stunned, too much like one escaped from a belfry on a coronation day. I am just resting from the fatigue of four days' hard listening--four snowy, sleety, rainy days; days of every variety of falling weather, all of them too bad to admit the possibility that any petticoated thing, were she as hardy as a Scotch fir, should stir out; four days chained by 'sad civility' to that fireside, once so quiet, and again--cheering thought!--again I trust to be so when the echo of that visitor's incessant tongue shall have died away....

"She took us in her way from London to the west of England, and being, as she wrote, 'not quite well, not equal to much company, prayed that no other guest might be admitted, so that she might have the pleasure of our conversation all to herself (ours! as if it were possible for any of us to slide in a word edgewise!), and especially enjoy the gratification of talking over old times with the master of the house, her countryman.'

"Such was the promise of her letter, and to the letter it has been kept. All the news and scandal of a large county forty years ago, and a hundred years before, and ever since; all the marriages, deaths, births, elopements, law-suits, and casualties of her own times, her father's, grandfather's, great-grandfather's, nephews', and grandnephews', has she detailed with a minuteness, an accuracy, a prodigality of learning, a profuseness of proper names, a pedantry of locality, which would excite the envy of a county historian, a king-at-arms, or even a Scotch novelist.

"Her knowledge is most astonishing; but the most astonishing part of all is how she came by that knowledge. It should seem, to listen to her, as if at some time of her life she must have listened herself; and yet her countryman declares that in the forty years he has known her, no such event has occurred; and she knows new news, too! It must be intuition!...

"The very weather is not a safe subject. Her memory is a perpetual register of hard frosts and long droughts, and high winds and terrible storms, with all the evils that followed in their train, and all the personal events connected with them; so that, if you happen to remark that clouds are come up and you fear it may rain, she replies: 'Ay, it is just such a morning as three-and-thirty years ago, when my poor cousin was married--you remember my cousin Barbara; she married so-and-so, the son of so-and-so;' and then comes the whole pedigree of the bridegroom, the amount of the settlements, and the reading and signing them overnight; a description of the wedding-dresses in the style of Sir Charles Grandison, and how much the bride's gown cost per yard; the names, residences, and a short subsequent history of the bridesmaids and men, the gentleman who gave the bride away, and the clergyman who performed the ceremony, with a learned antiquarian digression relative to the church; then the setting out in procession; the marriage, the kissing, the crying, the breakfasting, the drawing the cake through the ring, and, finally, the bridal excursion, which brings us back again, at an hour's end, to the starting-post, the weather, and the whole story of the sopping, the drying, the clothes-spoiling, the cold-catching, and all the small evils of a summer shower. By this time it rains, and she sits down to a pathetic see-saw of conjectures on the chance of Mrs. Smith's having set out for her daily walk, or the possibility that Dr. Brown may have ventured to visit his patients in his gig, and the certainty that Lady Green's new housemaid would come from London on the outside of the coach....

"I wonder, if she had happened to be married, how many husbands she would have talked to death. It is certain that none of her relatives are long-lived, after she comes to reside with them. Father, mother, uncle, sister, brother, two nephews, and one niece, all these have successively passed away, though a healthy race, and with no visible disorder--except--But we must not be uncharitable."

* * * * *

Mary Ferrier, the Scotch novelist, was gifted with genial wit and a quick sense of the ludicrous. Walter Scott admired her greatly, and as a lively guest at Abbotsford she did much to relieve the sadness of his last days. He said of her:

"She is a gifted personage, having, besides her great talents, conversation the least exigeante of any author, female at least, whom I have ever seen, among the long list I have encountered. Simple and full of humor, and exceedingly ready at repartee; and all this without the least affectation of the blue-stocking. The general strain of her writing relates to the foibles and oddities of mankind, and no one has drawn them with greater breadth of comic humor or effect. Her scenes often resemble the style of our best old comedies, and she may boast, like Foote, of adding many new and original characters to the stock of our comic literature."

Here is one of her admirably-drawn portraits:

THE SENSIBLE WOMAN.

"Miss Jacky, the senior of the trio, was what is reckoned a very sensible woman--which generally means a very disagreeable, obstinate, illiberal director of all men, women, and children--a sort of superintendent of all actions, time, and place, with unquestioned authority to arraign, judge, and condemn upon the statutes of her own supposed sense. Most country parishes have their sensible woman, who lays down the law on all affairs, spiritual and temporal. Miss Jacky stood unrivalled as the sensible woman of Glenfern. She had attained this eminence partly from having a little more understanding than her sisters, but principally from her dictatorial manner, and the pompous, decisive tone in which she delivered the most commonplace truths. At home her supremacy in all matters of sense was perfectly established; and thence the infection, like other superstitions, had spread over the whole neighborhood. As a sensible woman she regulated the family, which she took care to let everybody hear; she was a sort of postmistress-general, a detector of all abuses and impositions, and deemed it her prerogative to be consulted about all the useful and useless things which everybody else could have done as well. She was liberal of her advice to the poor, always enforcing upon them the iniquity of idleness, but doing nothing for them in the way of employment, strict economy being one of the many points in which she was particularly sensible. The consequence was that, while she was lecturing half the poor women in the parish for their idleness, the bread was kept out of their mouths by the incessant carding of wool, and knitting of stockings, and spinning, and reeling, and winding, and pirning, that went on among the ladies themselves. And, by the by, Miss Jacky is not the only sensible woman who thinks she is acting a meritorious part when she converts what ought to be the portion of the poor into the employment of the affluent.

"In short, Min Jacky was all over sense. A skilful physiognomist would at a single glance have detected the sensible woman in the erect head, the compressed lips, square elbows, and firm, judicious step. Even her very garments seemed to partake of the prevailing character of their mistress. Her ruff always looked more sensible than any other body's; her shawl sat most sensibly on her shoulders; her walking-shoes were acknowledged to be very sensible, and she drew on her gloves with an air of sense, as if the one arm had been Seneca, the other Socrates. From what has been said it may easily be inferred that Miss Jacky was, in fact, anything but a sensible woman, as, indeed, no woman can be who bears such visible outward marks of what is in reality the most quiet and unostentatious of all good qualities."

* * * * *

Frederika Bremer, the Swedish novelist, whose novels have been translated into English, German, French, and Dutch, had a style peculiarly her own. Her humor reminds me of a bed of mignonette, with its delicate yet permeating fragrance. One paragraph, like one spray of that shy flower, scarcely reveals the dainty flavor.

From the "Neighbors," her best story, and one that still has a moderate sale, I take her description of Franziska's first little lover-like quarrel with her adoring husband, the "Bear." (Let us remember Miss Bremer with appreciation and gratitude, as one of the very few visitors we have entertained who have written kindly of our country and our "Homes.")

THE FIRST QUARREL.

"Here I am again sitting with a pen in my hand, impelled by a desire for writing, yet with nothing particular to write about. Everything in the house and in the whole household arrangement is in order. Little patties are baking in the kitchen, the weather is oppressively hot, and every leaf and bird seem as if deprived of motion. The hens lie outside in the sand before the window, the cock stands solitarily on one leg, and looks upon his harem with the countenance of a sleepy sultan. Bear sits in his room writing letters. I hear him yawn; that infects me. Oh! oh! I must go and have a little quarrel with him on purpose to awaken us both.

"I want at this moment a quire of writing-paper on which to drop sugar-cakes. He is terribly miserly of his writing-paper, and on that very account I must have some now.

"Later.--All is done! A complete quarrel, and how completely lively we are after it! You, Maria, must hear all, that you may thus see how it goes on among married people.

"I went to my husband and said quite meekly, 'My Angel Bear, you must be so very good as to give me a quire of your writing-paper to drop sugar-cakes upon.'

"He (in consternation). 'A quire of writing-paper?'

"She. 'Yes, my dear friend, of your very best writing-paper.'

"He. 'Finest writing-paper? Are you mad?'

"She. 'Certainly not; but I believe you are a little out of your senses.'

"He. 'You covetous sea-cat, leave off raging among my papers! You shall not have my paper!'

"She. 'Miserly beast! I shall and will have the paper.'

"He. '"I shall"! Listen a moment. Let's see, now, how you will accomplish your will.' And the rough Bear held both my small hands fast in his great paws.

"She. 'You ugly Bear! You are worse than any of those that walk on four legs. Let me loose! Let me loose, else I shall bite you!' And as he would not let me loose I bit him. Yes, Maria, I bit him really on the hand, at which he only laughed scornfully and said: 'Yes, yes, my little wife, that is always the way of those who are forward without the power to do. Take the paper. Now, take it!'

"She. 'Ah! Let me loose! let me loose!'

"He. 'Ask me prettily.'

"She. 'Dear Bear!'

"He. 'Acknowledge your fault.'

"She. 'I do.'

"He. 'Pray for forgiveness.'

"She. 'Ah, forgiveness!'

"He. 'Promise amendment.'

"She. 'Oh, yes, amendment!'

"He. 'Nay, I'll pardon you. But now, no sour faces, dear wife, but throw your arms round my neck and kiss me.'

"I gave him a little box on the ear, stole a quire of paper, and ran off with loud exultation. Bear followed into the kitchen growling horribly; but then I turned upon him armed with two delicious little patties, which I aimed at his mouth, and there they vanished. Bear, all at once, was quite still, the paper was forgotten, and reconciliation concluded.

"There is, Maria, no better way of stopping the mouths of these lords of the creation than by putting into them something good to eat."

* * * * *

I wish I had room for my favorite Irishwoman, Lady Morgan, and her description of her first rout at the house of the eccentric Lady Cork.

The off-hand songs of her sister, Lady Clarke, are fine illustrations of rollicking Irish wit and badinage.

At one of Lady Morgan's receptions, given in honor of fifty philosophers from England, Lady Clarke sang the following song with "great effect:"

FUN AND PHILOSOPHY.

Heigh for ould Ireland! Oh, would you require a land Where men by nature are all quite the thing, Where pure inspiration has taught the whole nation To fight, love, and reason, talk politics, sing; 'Tis Pat's mathematical, chemical, tactical, Knowing and practical, fanciful, gay, Fun and philosophy, supping and sophistry, There's nothing in life that is out of his way.

He makes light of optics, and sees through dioptrics, He's a dab at projectiles--ne'er misses his man; He's complete in attraction, and quick at reaction, By the doctrine of chances he squares every plan; In hydraulics so frisky, the whole Bay of Biscay, If it flowed but with whiskey, he'd store it away. Fun and philosophy, supping and sophistry, There's nothing in life that is out of his way.

So to him cross over savant and philosopher, Thinking, God help them! to bother us all; But they'll find that for knowledge 'tis at our own college Themselves must inquire for--beds, dinner, or ball. There are lectures to tire, and good lodgings to hire, To all who require and have money to pay; While fun and philosophy, supping and sophistry, Ladies and lecturing fill up the day.

So at the Rotunda we all sorts of fun do, Hard hearts and pig-iron we melt in one flame; For if Love blows the bellows, our tough college fellows Will thaw into rapture at each lovely dame. There, too, sans apology, tea, tarts, tautology, Are given with zo 鰈 ogy, to grave and gay; Thus fun and philosophy, supping and sophistry Send all to England home, happy and gay.

* * * * *

From George Eliot, whose humor is seen at its best in "Adam Bede" and

"Silas Marner," how much we could quote! How some of her searching comments cling to the memory!

"I've nothing to say again' her piety, my dear; but I know very well I shouldn't like her to cook my victuals. When a man comes in hungry and tired, piety won't feed him, I reckon. Hard carrots 'ull lie heavy on his stomach, piety or no piety. I called in one day when she was dishin' up Mr. Tryan's dinner, an' I could see the potatoes was as watery as watery. It's right enough to be speritial, I'm no enemy to that, but I like my potatoes mealy."

"You're right there, Tookey; there's allays two 'pinions: there's the 'pinion a man has of himsen, and there's the 'pinion other folks have on him. There'd be two 'pinions about a cracked bell if the bell could hear itself."

"You're mighty fond o' Craig; but for my part, I think he's welly like a cock as thinks the sun's rose o' purpose to hear him crow."

"When Mr. Brooke had something painful to tell it was usually his way to introduce it among a number of disjointed particulars, as if it were a medicine that would get a milder flavor by mixing."

"Heaven knows what would become of our sociality if we never visited people we speak ill of; we should live like Egyptian hermits, in crowded solitude."

"No, I ain't one to see the cat walking into the dairy and wonder what she's come after."

"I have nothing to say again' Craig, on'y it is a pity he couldna be hatched o'er again, and hatched different."

"I'm not denyin' the women are foolish; God Almighty made 'em to match the men."

"It's a waste of time to praise people dead whom you maligned while living; for it's but a poor harvest you'll get by watering last year's crop."

"I suppose Dinah's like all the rest of the women, and thinks two and two will come to make five, if she only cries and makes bother enough about it."

"Put a good face on it and don't seem to be looking out for crows, else you'll set other people to watchin' for 'em, too."

"I took pretty good care, before I said 'sniff,' to be sure she would say 'snaff,' and pretty quick, too. I warn't a-goin' to open my mouth like a dog at a fly, and snap it to again wi' nothin' to swaller."

CHAPTER III.

FROM ANNE BRADSTREET TO MRS. STOWE.

The same gratifying progress and improvement noticed in the wit of women of other lands is seen in studying the literary annals of our own countrywomen.

Think of Anne Bradstreet, Mercy Warren, and Tabitha Tenney, all extolled to the skies by their contemporaries.

* * * * *

Mercy Warren was a satirist quite in the strain of Juvenal, but in cumbrous, artificial fashion.

Hon. John Winthrop consulted her on the proposed suspension of trade with England in all but the necessaries of life, and she playfully gives a list of articles that would be included in that word:

"An inventory clear Of all she needs Lamira offers here; Nor does she fear a rigid Cato's frown, When she lays by the rich embroidered gown, And modestly compounds for just enough, Perhaps some dozens of mere flighty stuff; With lawns and lute strings, blonde and Mechlin laces, Fringes and jewels, fans and tweezer-cases; Gay cloaks and hat, of every shape and size, Scarfs, cardinals, and ribands, of all dyes, With ruffles stamped and aprons of tambour, Tippets and handkerchiefs, at least threescore; With finest muslins that fair India boasts, And the choice herbage from Chinesian coasts; Add feathers, furs, rich satin, and ducapes, And head-dresses in pyramidal shapes;

Sideboards of plate and porcelain profuse, With fifty dittoes that the ladies use. So weak Lamira and her wants so few Who can refuse? they're but the sex's due."

* * * * *

Mrs. Sigourney, voluminous and mediocre, is amusing because so absolutely destitute of humor, and her style, a feminine Johnsonese, is absurdly hifalutin and strained.

This is the way in which she alludes to green apples:

"From the time of their first taking on orbicular shape, and when it might be supposed their hardness and acidity would repulse all save elephantine tusks and ostrich stomachs, they were the prey of roaming children."

And in her poem "To a Shred of Linen":

"Methinks I scan Some idiosyncrasy that marks thee out A defunct pillow-case."

She preserved, however, a long list of the various solicitations sent her to furnish poems for special occasions, and I think this shows that she possessed a sense of humor. Let me quote a few:

"Some verses were desired as an elegy on a pet canary accidentally drowned in a barrel of swine's food.

"A poem requested on the dog-star Sirius.

"To write an ode for the wedding of people in Maine, of whom I had never heard.

"To punctuate a three-volume novel for an author who complained that the work of punctuating always brought on a pain in the small of his back.

"Asked to assist a servant-man not very well able to read in getting his Sunday-school lessons, and to write out all the answers for him clear through the book--to save his time.

"A lady whose husband expects to be absent on a journey for a month or two wishes I would write a poem to testify her joy at his return.

"An elegy on a young man, one of the nine children of a judge of probate."

* * * * *

Miss Sedgwick, in her letters, occasionally showed a keen sense of humor, as, when speaking of a certain novel, she said:

"There is too much force for the subject. It is as if a railroad should be built and a locomotive started to transport skeletons, specimens, and one bird of Paradise."

* * * * *

Mrs. Caroline Gilman, born in 1794, and still living, author of "Recollections of a Southern Matron," etc., will be represented by one playful poem, which has a veritable New England flavor:

JOSHUA'S COURTSHIP.

A NEW ENGLAND BALLAD.

Stout Joshua was a farmer's son, And a pondering he sat One night when the fagots crackling burned, And purred the tabby cat.

Joshua was a well-grown youth, As one might plainly see By the sleeves that vainly tried to reach His hands upon his knee.

His splay-feet stood all parrot-toed In cowhide shoes arrayed, And his hair seemed cut across his brow By rule and plummet laid.

And what was Joshua pondering on, With his widely staring eyes, And his nostrils opening sensibly To ease his frequent sighs?

Not often will a lover's lips The tender secret tell, But out he spoke before he thought, "My gracious! Nancy Bell!"

His mother at her spinning-wheel, Good woman, stood and spun, "And what," says she, "is come o'er you, Is't airnest or is't fun?"

Then Joshua gave a cunning look, Half bashful and half sporting, "Now what did father do," says he, "When first he came a courting?"

"Why, Josh, the first thing that he did," With a knowing wink, said she, "He dressed up of a Sunday night, And cast sheep's eyes at me."

Josh said no more, but straight went out And sought a butcher's pen, Where twelve fat sheep, for market bound, Had lately slaughtered been.

He bargained with a lover's zeal, Obtained the wished-for prize, And filled his pockets fore and aft With twice twelve bloody eyes.

The next night was the happy time When all New England sparks, Drest in their best, go out to court, As spruce and gay as larks.

When floors are nicely sanded o'er, When tins and pewter shine, And milk-pans by the kitchen wall Display their dainty line;

While the new ribbon decks the waist Of many a waiting lass, Who steals a conscious look of pride Toward her answering glass.

In pensive mood sat Nancy Bell; Of Joshua thought not she, But of a hearty sailor lad Across the distant sea.

Her arm upon the table rests, Her hand supports her head, When Joshua enters with a scrape, And somewhat bashful tread.

No word he spake, but down he sat, And heaved a doleful sigh, Then at the table took his aim And rolled a glassy eye.

Another and another flew, With quick and strong rebound, They tumbled in poor Nancy's lap, They fell upon the ground.

While Joshua smirked, and sighed, and smiled Between each tender aim, And still the cold and bloody balls In frightful quickness came.

Until poor Nancy flew with screams, To shun the amorous sport, And Joshua found to cast sheep's eyes Was not the way to court.

* * * * *

"Fanny Forrester" and "Fanny Fern" both delighted the public with individual styles of writing, vastly successful when a new thing.

When wanting a new dress and bonnet, as every woman will in the spring (or any time), Fanny Forrester wrote to Willis, of the New Mirror, an appeal which he called "very clever, adroit, and fanciful."

"You know the shops in Broadway are very tempting this season. Such beautiful things! Well, you know (no, you don't know that, but you can guess) what a delightful thing it would be to appear in one of those charming, head-adorning, complexion-softening, hard-feature-subduing Neapolitans, with a little gossamer veil dropping daintily on the shoulder of one of those exquisite balzarines, to be seen any day at Stewart's and elsewhere. Well, you know (this you must know) that shopkeepers have the impertinence to demand a trifling exchange for these things, even of a lady; and also that some people have a remarkably small purse, and a remarkably small portion of the yellow "root" in that. And now, to bring the matter home, I am one of that class. I have the most beautiful little purse in the world, but it is only kept for show. I even find myself under the necessity of counterfeiting--that is, filling the void with tissue-paper in lieu of bank-notes, preparatory to a shopping expedition. Well, now to the point. As Bel and I snuggled down on the sofa this morning to read the New Mirror (by the way, Cousin Bel is never obliged to put tissue-paper in her purse), it struck us that you would be a friend in need, and give good counsel in this emergency. Bel, however, insisted on my not telling what I wanted the money for. She even thought that I had better intimate orphanage, extreme suffering from the bursting of some speculative bubble, illness, etc.; but did I not know you better? Have I read the New Mirror so much (to say nothing of the graceful things coined under a bridge, and a thousand other pages flung from the inner heart) and not learned who has an eye for everything pretty? Not so stupid, Cousin Bel, no, no!...

"And to the point. Maybe you of the New Mirror PAY for acceptable articles, maybe not. Comprenez vous? Oh, I do hope that beautiful balzarine like Bel's will not be gone before another Saturday! You will not forget to answer me in the next Mirror; but pray, my dear Editor, let it be done very cautiously, for Bel would pout all day if she should know what I have written.

"Till Saturday, your anxiously-waiting friend,

"FANNY FORRESTER."

Such a note received by an editor of this generation would promptly fall into the waste-basket. But Willis was captivated, and answered:

"Well, we give in! On condition that you are under twenty-five and that you will wear a rose (recognizably) in your bodice the first time you appear in Broadway with the hat and balzarine, we will pay the bills. Write us thereafter a sketch of Bel and yourself as cleverly done as this letter, and you may 'snuggle' down on the sofa and consider us paid, and the public charmed with you."

This style of ingratiating one's self with an editor is as much a bygone as an alliterative pen-name.

* * * * *

Fanny Fern (Sarah Willis Parton) also established a style of her own--"a new kind of composition; short, pointed paragraphs, without beginning and without end--one clear, ringing note, and then silence."

Her talent for humorous composition showed itself in her essays at school. I'll give a bit from her "Suggestions on Arithmetic after Cramming for an Examination":

"Every incident, every object of sight seemed to produce an arithmetical result. I once saw a poor wretch evidently intoxicated; thought I, 'That man has overcome three scruples, to say the least, for three scruples make one dram.' Even the Sabbath was no day of rest for me--the psalms, prayers, and sermons were all translated by me into the language of arithmetic. A good man spoke very feelingly upon the manner in which our cares and perplexities were multiplied by riches. Muttered I: 'That, sir, depends upon whether the multiplier is a fraction or a whole number; for if it be a fraction, it makes the product less.' And when another, lamenting the various divisions of the Church, pathetically exclaimed: 'And how shall we unite these several denominations in one?'

"'Why, reduce them to a common denominator,' exclaimed I, half aloud, wondering at his ignorance.

"And when an admiring swain protested his warm 'interest,' he brought only one word that chimed with my train of thought.

"'Interest?' exclaimed I, starting from my reverie. 'What per cent, sir?'

"'Ma'am?' exclaimed my attendant, in the greatest possible amazement.

"'How much per cent, sir?' said I, repeating my question.

"His reply was lost on my ear save: 'Madam, at any rate do not trifle with my feelings.'

"'At any rate, did you say? Then take six per cent; that is the easiest to calculate.'"

Her style, too, has gone out of fashion; but in its day it was thought very amusing.

* * * * *

Mrs. Stowe needs no introduction, and she is another of those from whom we quote little, because she could contribute so much, and one does not know where to choose. Her "Sam Lawson" is, perhaps, the most familiar of her odd characters and talkers.

SAM LAWSON'S SAYINGS.

"Well, Sam, what did you think of the sermon?" said Uncle Bill.

"Well," said Sam, leaning over the fire with his long, bony hands alternately raised to catch the warmth, and then dropped with an utter laxness when the warmth became too pronounced, "Parson Simpson's a smart man; but I tell ye, it's kind o' discouragin'. Why, he said our state and condition by natur war just like this: We war clear down in a well fifty feet deep, and the sides all round nothin' but glare ice; but we war under immediate obligations to get out, 'cause we war free, voluntary agents. But nobody ever had got out, and nobody would, unless the Lord reached down and took 'em. And whether he would or not nobody could tell; it was all sovereignty. He said there warn't one in a hundred, not one in a thousand, not one in ten thousand, that would be saved. 'Lordy massy,' says I to myself, 'ef that's so they're any of 'em welcome to my chance.' And so I kind o' ris up and come out, 'cause I'd got a pretty long walk home, and I wanted to go round by South Pond and inquire about Aunt Sally Morse's toothache."...

"This 'ere Miss Sphyxy Smith's a rich old gal, and 'mazin' smart to work," he began. "Tell you, she holds all she gets. Old Sol, he told me a story 'bout her that was a pretty good un."

"What was it?" said my grandmother.

"Wal, ye see, you 'member old Parson Jeduthun Kendall that lives up in Stonytown; he lost his wife a year ago last Thanksgivin', and he thought 'twar about time he hed another; so he comes down and consults our Parson Lothrop. Says he: 'I want a good, smart, neat, economical woman, with a good property. I don't care nothin' about her bein' handsome. In fact, I ain't particular about anything else,' says he. Wal, Parson Lothrop, says he: 'I think, if that's the case, I know jest the woman to suit ye. She owns a clear, handsome property, and she's neat and economical; but she's no beauty!' 'Oh, beauty is nothin' to me,' says Parson Kendall; and so he took the direction. Wal, one day he hitched up his old one-hoss shay, and kind o' brushed up, and started off a-courtin'. Wal, the parson come to the house, and he war tickled to pieces with the looks o' things outside, 'cause the house is all well shingled and painted, and there ain't a picket loose nor a nail wantin' nowhere.

"'This 'ere's the woman for me,' says Parson Kendall. So he goes up and raps hard on the front door with his whip-handle. Wal, you see, Miss Sphyxy she war jest goin' out to help get in her hay. She had on a pair o' clompin' cowhide boots, and a pitchfork in her hand, jest goin' out, when she heard the rap. So she come jest as she was to the front door. Now, you know Parson Kendall's a little midget of a man, but he stood there on the step kind o' smilin' and genteel, lickin' his lips and lookin' so agreeable! Wal, the front door kind o' stuck--front doors generally do, ye know, 'cause they ain't opened very often--and Miss Sphyxy she had to pull and haul and put to all her strength, and finally it come open with a bang, and she 'peared to the parson, pitchfork and all, sort o' frownin' like.

"'What do you want?' says she; for, you see, Miss Sphyxy ain't no ways tender to the men.

"'I want to see Miss Asphyxia Smith,' says he, very civil, thinking she war the hired gal.

"'I'm Miss Asphyxia Smith,' says she. 'What do you want o' me?'

"Parson Kendall he jest took one good look on her, from top to toe. 'NOTHIN',' says he, and turned right round and went down the steps like lightnin'."

* * * * *

Years ago Mrs. Stowe published some capital stories of New England life, which were collected in a little volume called "The Mayflower," a book which is now seldom seen, and almost unknown to the present generation. From this I take her "Night in a Canal-Boat." Extremely effective when read with enthusiasm and proper variety of tone. I quote it as a boon for the boys and girls who are often looking for something "funny" to read aloud.

THE CANAL-BOAT.

BY HARRIET BEECHER STOWE.

Of all the ways of travelling which obtain among our locomotive nation, this said vehicle, the canal-boat, is the most absolutely prosaic and inglorious. There is something picturesque, nay, almost sublime, in the lordly march of your well-built, high-bred steamboat. Go take your stand on some overhanging bluff, where the blue Ohio winds its thread of silver, or the sturdy Mississippi tears its path through unbroken forests, and it will do your heart good to see the gallant boat walking the waters with unbroken and powerful tread, and, like some fabled monster of the wave, breathing fire and making the shores resound with its deep respirations. Then there is something mysterious--even awful--in the power of steam. See it curling up against a blue sky some rosy morning, graceful, floating, intangible, and to all appearance the softest and gentlest of all spiritual things, and then think that it is this fairy spirit that keeps all the world alive and hot with motion; think how excellent a servant it is, doing all sorts of gigantic works, like the genii of old; and yet, if you let slip the talisman only for a moment, what terrible advantage it will take of you! and you will confess that steam has some claims both to the beautiful and the terrible! For our own part, when we are down among the machinery of a steamboat in full play, we conduct ourselves very reverently, for we consider it as a very serious neighborhood, and every time the steam whizzes with such red-hot determination from the escape-valve, we start as if some of the spirits were after us. But in a canal-boat there is no power, no mystery, no danger; one cannot blow up, one cannot be drowned-- unless by some special effort; one sees clearly all there is in the case--a horse, a rope, and a muddy strip of water--and that is all.

Did you ever try it, reader? If not, take an imaginary trip with us, just for experiment. "There's the boat!" exclaims a passenger in the omnibus, as we are rolling down from the Pittsburg Mansion House to the canal. "Where?" exclaim a dozen of voices, and forthwith a dozen heads go out of the window. "Why, down there, under that bridge; don't you see those lights?" "What, that little thing!" exclaims an inexperienced traveller; "dear me! we can't half of us get into it!" "We! indeed," says some old hand in the business; "I think you'll find it will hold us and a dozen more loads like us." "Impossible!" say some. "You'll see," say the initiated; and as soon as you get out you do see, and hear, too, what seems like a general breaking loose from the Tower of Babel, amid a perfect hail-storm of trunks, boxes, valises, carpet-bags, and every describable and indescribable form of what a Westerner calls "plunder."

"That's my trunk!" barks out a big, round man. "That's my bandbox!" screams a heart-stricken old lady, in terror for her immaculate Sunday caps. "Where's my little red box? I had two carpet-bags and a--My trunk had a scarle--Halloo! where are you going with that portmanteau? Husband! Husband! do see after the large basket and the little hair-trunk--Oh, and the baby's little chair!" "Go below, go below, for mercy's sake, my dear; I'll see to the baggage." At last the feminine part of creation, perceiving that, in this particular instance, they gain nothing by public speaking, are content to be led quietly under hatches; and amusing is the look of dismay which each new-comer gives to the confined quarters that present themselves. Those who were so ignorant of the power of compression as to suppose the boat scarce large enough to contain them and theirs, find, with dismay, a respectable colony of old ladies, babies, mothers, big baskets, and carpet-bags already established. "Mercy on us!" says one, after surveying the little room, about ten feet long and six feet high, "where are we all to sleep to-night?" "Oh, me, what a sight of children!" says a young lady, in a despairing tone. "Pooh!" says an initiated traveller, "children! scarce any here; let's see: one; the woman in the corner, two; that child with the bread and butter, three; and then there's that other woman with two. Really, it's quite moderate for a canal-boat. However, we can't tell till they have all come."

"All! for mercy's sake, you don't say there are any more coming!" exclaim two or three in a breath; "they can't come; there is not room!"

Notwithstanding the impressive utterance of this sentence the contrary is immediately demonstrated by the appearance of a very corpulent elderly lady with three well-grown daughters, who come down looking about them most complacently, entirely regardless of the unchristian looks of the company. What a mercy it is that fat people are always good-natured!

After this follows an indiscriminate raining down of all shapes, sizes, sexes, and ages--men, women, children, babies, and nurses. The state of feeling becomes perfectly desperate. Darkness gathers on all faces. "We shall be smothered! we shall be crowded to death! we can't stay here!" are heard faintly from one and another; and yet, though the boat grows no wider, the walls no higher, they do live, and do stay there, in spite of repeated protestations to the contrary. Truly, as Sam Slick says, "there's a sight of wear in human natur'!"

But meanwhile the children grow sleepy, and divers interesting little duets and trios arise from one part or another of the cabin.

"Hush, Johnny! be a good boy," says a pale, nursing mamma, to a great, bristling, white-headed phenomenon, who is kicking very much at large in her lap.

"I won't be a good boy, neither," responds Johnny, with interesting explicitness; "I want to go to bed, and so-o-o-o!" and Johnny makes up a mouth as big as a tea-cup, and roars with good courage, and his mamma asks him "if he ever saw pa do so," and tells him that "he is mamma's dear, good little boy, and must not make a noise," with various observations of the kind, which are so strikingly efficacious in such cases. Meanwhile the domestic concert in other quarters proceeds with vigor. "Mamma, I'm tired!" bawls a child. "Where's the baby's nightgown?" calls a nurse. "Do take Peter up in your lap, and keep him still." "Pray get out some biscuits to stop their mouths." Meanwhile sundry babies strike in con spirito, as the music-books have it, and execute various flourishes; the disconsolate mothers sigh, and look as if all was over with them; and the young ladies appear extremely disgusted, and wonder "what business women have to be travelling round with children."

To these troubles succeeds the turning-out scene, when the whole caravan is ejected into the gentlemen's cabin, that the beds may be made. The red curtains are put down, and in solemn silence all the last mysterious preparations begin. At length it is announced that all is ready. Forthwith the whole company rush back, and find the walls embellished by a series of little shelves, about a foot wide, each furnished with a mattress and bedding, and hooked to the ceiling by a very suspiciously slender cord. Direful are the ruminations and exclamations of inexperienced travellers, particularly young ones, as they eye these very equivocal accommodations. "What, sleep up there! I won't sleep on one of those top shelves, I know. The cords will certainly break." The chambermaid here takes up the conversation, and solemnly assures them that such an accident is not to be thought of at all; that it is a natural impossibility--a thing that could not happen without an actual miracle; and since it becomes increasingly evident that thirty ladies cannot all sleep on the lowest shelf, there is some effort made to exercise faith in this doctrine; nevertheless all look on their neighbors with fear and trembling; and when the stout lady talks of taking a shelf, she is most urgently pressed to change places with her alarmed neighbor below. Points of location being after a while adjusted, comes the last struggle. Everybody wants to take off a bonnet, or look for a shawl, to find a cloak, or get a carpet-bag, and all set about it with such zeal that nothing can be done. "Ma'am, you're on my foot!" says one. "Will you please to move, ma'am?" says somebody, who is gasping and struggling behind you. "Move!" you echo. "Indeed, I should be very glad to, but I don't see much prospect of it." "Chambermaid!" calls a lady who is struggling among a heap of carpet-bags and children at one end of the cabin. "Ma'am!" echoes the poor chambermaid, who is wedged fast in a similar situation at the other. "Where's my cloak, chambermaid?" "I'd find it, ma'am, if I could move." "Chambermaid, my basket!" "Chambermaid, my parasol!" "Chambermaid, my carpet-bag!" "Mamma, they push me so!" "Hush, child; crawl under there and lie still till I can undress you." At last, however, the various distresses are over, the babies sink to sleep, and even that much-enduring being, the chambermaid, seeks out some corner for repose. Tired and drowsy, you are just sinking into a doze, when bang! goes the boat against the sides of a lock; ropes scrape, men run and shout; and up fly the heads of all the top-shelfites, who are generally the more juvenile and airy part of the company.

"What's that! what's that!" flies from mouth to mouth; and forthwith they proceed to awaken their respective relations. "Mother! Aunt Hannah! do wake up; what is this awful noise?" "Oh, only a lock." "Pray, be still," groan out the sleepy members from below.

"A lock!" exclaim the vivacious creatures, ever on the alert for information; "and what is a lock, pray?"

"Don't you know what a lock is, you silly creatures. Do lie down and go to sleep."

"But say, there ain't any danger in a lock, is there?" respond the querists. "Danger!" exclaims a deaf old lady, poking up her head. "What's the matter? There hain't nothing burst, has there?" "No, no, no!" exclaim the provoked and despairing opposition party, who find that there is no such thing as going to sleep till they have made the old lady below and the young ladies above understand exactly the philosophy of a lock. After a while the conversation again subsides; again all is still; you hear only the trampling of horses and the rippling of the rope in the water, and sleep again is stealing over you. You doze, you dream, and all of a sudden you are startled by a cry, "Chambermaid! wake up the lady that wants to be set ashore." Up jumps chambermaid, and up jump the lady and two children, and forthwith form a committee of inquiry as to ways and means. "Where's my bonnet?" says the lady, half awake and fumbling among the various articles of that name. "I thought I hung it up behind the door." "Can't you find it?" says the poor chambermaid, yawning and rubbing her eyes. "Oh, yes, here it is," says the lady; and then the cloak, the shawl, the gloves, the shoes, receive each a separate discussion. At last all seems ready, and they begin to move off, when lo! Peter's cap is missing. "Now, where can it be?" soliloquizes the lady. "I put it right here by the table-leg; maybe it got into some of the berths." At this suggestion the chambermaid takes the candle, and goes round deliberately to every berth, poking the light directly in the face of every sleeper. "Here it is," she exclaims, pulling at something black under one pillow. "No, indeed, those are my shoes," says the vexed sleeper. "Maybe it's here," she resumes, darting upon something dark in another berth. "No, that's my bag," responds the occupant. The chambermaid then proceeds to turn over all the children on the floor, to see if it is not under them. In the course of which process they are most agreeably waked up and enlivened; and when everybody is broad awake, and most uncharitably wishing the cap, and Peter too, at the bottom of the canal, the good lady exclaims, "Well, if this isn't lucky; here I had it safe in my basket all the time!" And she departed amid the--what shall I say? execrations!--of the whole company, ladies though they be.

Well, after this follows a hushing up and wiping up among the juvenile population, and a series of remarks commences from the various shelves of a very edifying and instructive tendency. One says that the woman did not seem to know where anything was; another says that she has waked them all up; a third adds that she has waked up all the children, too; and the elderly ladies make moral reflections on the importance of putting your things where you can find them--being always ready; which observations, being delivered in an exceedingly doleful and drowsy tone, form a sort of sub-bass to the lively chattering of the upper-shelfites, who declare that they feel quite awake--that they don't think they shall go to sleep again to-night, and discourse over everything in creation, until you heartily wish you were enough related to them to give them a scolding.

At last, however, voice after voice drops off; you fall into a most refreshing slumber; it seems to you that you sleep about a quarter of an hour, when the chambermaid pulls you by the sleeve. "Will you please to get up, ma'am? We want to make the beds." You start and stare. Sure enough, the night is gone. So much for sleeping on board canal-boats!

Let us not enumerate the manifold perplexities of the morning toilet in a place where every lady realizes most forcibly the condition of the old woman who lived under a broom: "All she wanted was elbow-room." Let us not tell how one glass is made to answer for thirty fair faces, one ewer and vase for thirty lavations; and--tell it not in Gath--one towel for a company! Let us not intimate how ladies' shoes have, in a night, clandestinely slid into the gentlemen's cabin, and gentlemen's boots elbowed, or, rather, toed their way among ladies' gear, nor recite the exclamations after runaway property that are heard.

"I can't find nothing of Johnny's shoe!" "Here's a shoe in the water-pitcher--is this it?" "My side-combs are gone!" exclaims a nymph with dishevelled curls. "Massy! do look at my bonnet!" exclaims an old lady, elevating an article crushed into as many angles as there are pieces in a mince-pie. "I never did sleep so much together in my life," echoes a poor little French lady, whom despair has driven into talking English.

But our shortening paper warns us not to prolong our catalogue of distresses beyond reasonable bounds, and therefore we will close with advising all our friends, who intend to try this way of travelling for pleasure, to take a good stock both of patience and clean towels with them, for we think that they will find abundant need for both.

CHAPTER IV.

"SAMPLES" HERE AND THERE.

Next comes Mrs. Caroline M. Kirkland with her Western sketches. Many will remember her laughable description of "Borrowing Out West," with its two appropriate mottoes: "Lend me your ears," from Shakespeare, and from Bacon: "Grant graciously what you cannot refuse safely."

"'Mother wants your sifter,' said Miss Ianthe Howard, a young lady of six years' standing, attired in a tattered calico thickened with dirt; her unkempt locks straggling from under that hideous substitute for a bonnet so universal in the Western country--a dirty cotton handkerchief--which is used ad nauseam for all sorts of purposes.

"'Mother wants your sifter, and she says she guesses you can let her have some sugar and tea, 'cause you've got plenty.' This excellent reason, ''cause you've got plenty,' is conclusive as to sharing with neighbors.

"Sieves, smoothing-irons, and churns run about as if they had legs; one brass kettle is enough for a whole neighborhood, and I could point to a cradle which has rocked half the babies in Montacute.

"For my own part, I have lent my broom, my thread, my tape, my spoons, my cat, my thimble, my scissors, my shawl, my shoes, and have been asked for my combs and brushes, and my husband for his shaving apparatus and pantaloons."

Mrs. Whither, whose "Widow Bedott" is a familiar name, resembles Mrs. Kirkland in her comic portraitures, which were especially good of their kind, and never betrayed any malice. The "Bedott Papers" first appeared in 1846, and became popular at once. They are good examples of what they simply profess to be: an amusing series of comicalities.

I shall not quote from them, as every one who enjoys that style of humor knows them by heart. It would be as useless as copying "Now I lay me down to sleep," or "Mary had a little lamb," for a child's collection of verses!

* * * * *

There are many authors whom I cannot represent worthily in these brief limits. When, encouraged by the unprecedented popularity of this venture, I prepare an encyclop 鎊 ia of the "Wit and Humor of American Women," I can do justice to such writers as "Gail Hamilton" and Miss Alcott, whose "Transcendental Wild Oats" cannot be cut. Rose Terry Cooke thinks her "Knoware" the only funny thing she has ever done. She is greatly mistaken, as I can soon prove. "Knoware" ought to be printed by itself to delight thousands, as her "Deacon's Week" has already done. To search for a few good things in the works of my witty friends is searching not for the time-honored needle in a hay-mow, but for two or three needles of just the right size out of a whole paper of needles.

"The Insanity of Cain," by Mrs. Mary Mapes Dodge, an inimitable satire on the feebleness of our jury system and the absurd pretence of "temporary insanity," must wait for that encyclop 蟲 ia. And her "Miss Molony on the Chinese Question" is known and admired by every one, including the Prince of Wales, who was fairly convulsed by its fun, when brought out by our favorite elocutionist, Miss Sarah Cowell, who had the honor of reading before royalty.

I regretfully omit the "Peterkin Letters," by Lucretia P. Hale, and time famous "William Henry Letters," by Mrs. Abby Morton Diaz. The very best bit from Miss Sallie McLean would be how "Grandma Spicer gets Grandpa Ready for Sunday-school," from the "Cape Cod Folks;" but why not save space for what is not in everybody's mouth and memory? This is equally true of Mrs. Cleaveland's "No Sects in Heaven," which, like Arabella Wilson's "Sextant," goes the rounds of all the papers every other year as a fresh delight.

Marietta Holley, too, must be allowed only a brief quotation. "Samantha" is a family friend from Mexico to Alaska. Mrs. Metta Victoria Victor, who died recently, has written an immense amount of humorous sketches. Her "Miss Slimmens," the boarding-house keeper, is a marked character, and will be remembered by many.

I will select a few "samples," unsatisfactory because there is so much more just as good, and then give room for others less familiar.

MISS LUCINDA'S PIG.

BY ROSE TERRY COOKE.

"You don't know of any poor person who'd like to have a pig, do you?" said Miss Lucinda, wistfully.

"Well, the poorer they was, the quicker they'd eat him up, I guess--ef they could eat such a razor-back."

"Oh, I don't like to think of his being eaten! I wish he could be got rid of some other way. Don't you think he might be killed in his sleep, Israel?"

"I think it's likely it would wake him up," said he, demurely. "Killin' 's killin', and a critter can't sleep over it 's though 'twas the stomachache. I guess he'd kick some, ef he was asleep--and screech some, too!"

"Dear me!" said Miss Lucinda, horrified at the idea. "I wish he could be sent out to run in the woods. Are there any good woods near here, Israel?"

"I don't know but what he'd as lieves be slartered to once as to starve an' be hunted down out in the lots. Besides, there ain't nobody as I knows of would like a hog to be a-rootin' round among their turnips and young wheat."

"Well, what I shall do with him I don't know!" despairingly exclaimed Miss Lucinda. "He was such a dear little thing when you bought him, Israel! Do you remember how pink his pretty little nose was--just like a rosebud--and how bright his eyes were, and his cunning legs? And now he's grown so big and fierce! But I can't help liking him, either."

"He's a cute critter, that's sartain; but he does too much rootin' to have a pink nose now, I expect; there's consider'ble on 't, so I guess it looks as well to have it gray. But I don't know no more'n you do what to do abaout it."

"If I could only get rid of him without knowing what became of him!" exclaimed Miss Lucinda, squeezing her forefinger with great earnestness, and looking both puzzled and pained.

"If Mees Lucinda would pairmit?" said a voice behind her.

She turned round to see Monsieur Leclerc on his crutches, just in the parlor-door.

"I shall, mees, myself dispose of piggie, if it please. I can. I shall have no sound; he shall to go away like a silent snow, to trouble you no more, never!"

"Oh, sir, if you could! But I don't see how!"

"If mees was to see, it would not be to save her pain. I shall have him to go by magique to fiery land."

Fairy-land, probably. But Miss Lucinda did not perceive the 閣 uivoque.

"Nor yet shall I trouble Meester Israyel. I shall have the aid of myself and one good friend that I have; and some night, when you rise of the morning, he shall not be there."

Miss Lucinda breathed a deep sigh of relief.

"I am greatly obliged--I mean, I shall be," said she.

"Well, I'm glad enough to wash my hands on 't," said Israel. "I shall hanker arter the critter some, but he's a-gettin' too big to be handy; 'n it's one comfort about critters, you ken git rid on 'em somehaow when they're more plague than profit. But folks has got to be let alone, excep' the Lord takes 'em; an' He generally don't see fit."--From Somebody's Neighbors.

A GIFT HORSE.

BY ROSE TERRY COOKE.

"Well, he no need to ha' done it, Sary. I've told him more'n four times he hadn't ought to pull a gun tow'rds him by the muzzle on't. Now he's up an' did it once for all."

"He won't never have no chance to do it again, Scotty, if you don't hurry up after the doctor," said Sary, wiping her eyes on her dirty calico apron, thereby adding an effective shadow under their redness.

"Well, I'm a-goin', ain't I? But ye know yerself 'twon't do to go so fur on eend, 'thout ye're vittled consider'ble well."

So saying, he fell to at the meal she had interrupted, hot potatoes, cold pork, dried venison, and blueberry pie vanishing down his throat with an alacrity and dispatch that augured well for the thorough "vittling" he intended, while Sary went about folding chunks of boiled ham, thick slices of brown bread, solid rounds of "sody biskit," and slab-sided turnovers in a newspaper, filling a flat bottle with whiskey, and now and then casting a look at the low bed where young Harry McAlister lay, very much whiter than the sheets about him, and quite as unconscious of surroundings, the blood oozing slowly through such bandages as Scott Peck's rude surgery had twisted about a gunshot-wound in his thigh, and brought to close tension by a stick thrust through the folds, turned as tight as could be borne, and strapped into place by a bit of coarse twine.

It was a long journey paddling up the Racquette River, across creek and carry, with the boat on his back, to the lakes, and then from Martin's to "Harri'tstown," where he knew a surgeon of repute from a great city was spending his vacation. It was touch-and-go with Harry before Scott and Dr. Drake got back. Sary had dosed him with venison-broth, hot and greasy, weak whiskey and water, and a little milk (only a little), for their cow was old and pastured chiefly on leaves and twigs, and she only came back to the shanty when she liked or needed to come, so their milk supply was uncertain, and Sary dared not leave her patient long enough to row to the end of Tupper's Lake, where the nearest cow was kept. But youth has a power of recovery that defies circumstance, and Dr. Drake was very skilful. Long weeks went by, and the green woods of July had brightened and faded into October's dim splendor before Harry McAlister could be carried up the river and over to Bartlett's, where his mother had been called to meet him. She was a widow, and he her only child; and, though she was rather silly and altogether unpractical, she had a tender, generous heart, and was ready to do anything possible for Scott and Sarah Peck to show her gratitude for their kindness to her boy. She did not consult Harry at all. He had lost much blood from his accident and recovered strength slowly. She kept everything like thought or trouble out of his way as far as she could, and when the family physician found her heart was set on taking him to Florida for the winter, because he looked pale and her grandmother's aunt had died of consumption, Dr. Peet, like a wise man, rubbed his hands together, bowed, and assured her it would be the very thing. But something must be done for the Pecks before she went away. It occurred to her how difficult it must be for them to row everywhere in a small boat. A horse would be much better. Even if the roads were not good they could ride, Sarah behind Scott. And so useful in farming, too. Her mind was made up at once. She dispatched a check for three hundred dollars to Peter Haas, her old coachman, who had bought a farm in Vermont with his savings, and retired, with the cook for his wife, into the private life of a farmer. Mrs. McAlister had much faith in Peter's knowledge of horses and his honesty. She wrote him to buy a strong, steady animal, and convey it to Scott Peck, either sending him word to come up to Bartlett's after it, or taking it down the river; but, at any rate, to make sure he had it. If the check would not pay all expenses, he was to draw on her for more. Peter took the opportunity to get rid of a horse he had no use for in winter; a beast restive as a racer when not in daily use, but strong enough for any work, and steady enough if he had work. Two hundred and fifty dollars was the price now set on his head, though Peter had bought him for seventy-five, and thought him dear at that. The remaining fifty was ample for expenses; but Peter was a prudent German and liked a margin. There was no difficulty in getting the horse as far as Martin's, and by dint of patient insistence Peter contrived to have him conveyed to Bartlett's; but here he rested and sent a messenger down to Scott Peck, while he himself returned to Bridget at the farm, slowly cursing the country and the people as he went his way, for his delays and troubles had been numerous.

"Gosh!" said Scott Peck, when he stepped up to the log-house that served for the guides, unknowing what awaited him, for the messenger had not found him at home, but left word he was to come to Bartlett's for something, and the first thing he saw was this gray horse.

"What fool fetched his hoss up here?"

The guides gathered about the door of their hut, burst into a loud cackle of laughter; even the beautiful hounds in their rough kennel leaped up and bayed.

"W-a-a-l;" drawled lazy Joe Tucker, "the feller 't owns him ain't nobody's fool. Be ye, Scotty?"

"Wha-t!" ejaculated Scott.

"It's your'n, man, sure as shootin'!" laughed Hearty Jack, Joe Tucker's brother.

"Mine? Jehoshaphat! Blaze that air track, will ye? I'm lost, sure."

"Well, Bartlett's gone out Keeseville way, so't kinder was lef' to me to tell ye. 'Member that ar chap that shot hisself in the leg down to your shanty this summer?"

"Well, I expect I do, seein' I ain't more'n a hundred year old," sarcastically answered Scott.

"He's cleared out South-aways some'eres, and his ma consaited she was dredful obleeged to ye; 'n I'm blessed if she didn't send an old Dutch feller up here fur to fetch ye that hoss fur a present. He couldn't noways wait to see ye pus'nally, he sed, fur he mistrusted the' was snows here sometimes 'bout this season. Ho! ho! ho!"

"Good land!" said Scott, sitting down on a log, and putting his hands in his pockets, the image of perplexity, while the men about him roared with fresh laughter. "What be I a-goin' to do with the critter?" he asked of the crowd.

"Blessed if I know," answered Hearty Jack.

"Can't ye get him out to 'Sable Falls or Keeseville 'n sell him fur what he'll fetch?" suggested Joe Tucker.

"I can't go now, noways. Sary's wood-pile's nigh gin out, 'n there was a mighty big sundog yesterday; 'nd moreover I smell snow. It'll be suthin' to git hum as 'tis. Mabbe Bartlett'll keep him a spell."

"No, he won't; you kin bet your head. His fodder's a-runnin' short for the hornid critters. He's bought some up to Martin's, that's a-comin' down dyrect; but 'tain't enough. He's put to't for more. Shouldn't wonder ef he had to draw from North Elby when sleddin' sets in."

"Well, I dono's there's but one thing for to do; fetch him hum somehow or 'nother; 'nd there's my boat over to the carry!"

"You'd better tie the critter on behind an' let him wade down the Racket!"

Another shout of laughter greeted this proposal.

"I s'all take ze boat for you!" quietly said a little brown Canadian--Jean Poiton. "I am go to Tupper to-morrow. I have one hunt to make. I can take her."

"Well said, Gene. I'll owe you a turn. But, fur all, how be I goin' to get that animile 'long the trail?"

"I dono!" answered Joe Tucker. "I expect, if it's got to be did, you'll fetch it somehow. But I'm mighty glad 'tain't my job!"

Scott Peck thought Joe had good reason for joy in that direction before he had gone a mile on his homeward way! The trail was only a trail, rough, devious, crossed with roots of trees, brushed with boughs of fir and pine, and the horse was restive and unruly. By nightfall he had gone only a few miles, and when he had tied the beast to a tree and covered him with a blanket brought from Bartlett's for the purpose, and strapped on his own back all the way, the light of the camp-fire startled the horse so that Scott was forced to blind him with a comforter before he would stand still. Then in the middle of the night, a great owl hooting from the tree-top just above him was a fresh scare, and but that the strap and rope both were new and strong he would have escaped. Scott listened to his rearing, trampling, snorts, and wild neigh with the composure of a sleepy man; but when he awoke at daylight, and found four inches of snow had fallen during the night, he swore.

This was too much. Even to his practised woodcraft it seemed impossible to get the horse safe to his clearing without harm. It was only by dint of the utmost care and patience, the greatest watchfulness of the way, that he got along at all. Every rod or two he stumbled, and all but fell himself. Here and there a loaded hemlock bough, weighed out of its uprightness by the wet snow, snapped in his face and blinded him with its damp burden; and he knew long before nightfall that another night in the woods was inevitable. He could feed the horse on young twigs of beech and birch; fresh moss, and new-peeled bark (fodder the animal would have resented with scorn under any other conditions); but hunger has no law concerning food. Scott himself was famished; but his pipe and tobacco were a refuge whose value he knew before, and his charge was tired enough to be quiet this second night; so the man had an undisturbed sleep by his comfortable fire. It was full noon of the next day when he reached his cabin. Jean Poiton had tied his boat to its stake, and gone on without stopping to speak to Sarah; so her surprise was wonderful when she saw Scott emerge from the forest, leading a gray creature, with drooping head and shambling gait, tired and dispirited.

"Heaven's to Betsey, Scott Peck! What hev you got theer?"

"The devil!" growled Scott.

Sary screamed.

"Do hold your jaw, gal, an' git me su'thin' hot to eat 'n drink. I'm savager'n an Injin. Come, git along." And, tying his horse to a stump, the hungry man followed Sarah into the house and helped himself out of a keg in the corner to a long, reviving draught.

"Du tell!" said Sarah, when the pork began to frizzle in the pan. "What upon airth did you buy a hoss for?" (She had discovered it was a horse.)

"Buy it! I guess not. I ain't no such blamed fool as that comes to. That feller you nussed up here a spell back, he up an' sent it roun' to Bartlett's, for a present to me."

"Well! Did he think you was a-goin' to set up canawl long o' Racket?"

"I expect he calc'lated I'd go racin'," dryly answered Scott.

"But what be ye a-goin' to feed him with?" said Sary, laying venison steaks into the pan.

"Lord knows! I don't. Shut up, Sary! I'm tuckered out with the beast. I'd ruther still-hunt three weeks on eend than fetch him in from Sar'nac, now I tell ye. Ain't them did enough? I could eat a raw bear."

Sary laughed and asked no more questions till the ravenous man had satisfied himself with the savory food; but, if she had asked them, Scott would have had no answer, for his mind was perplexed to the last degree. He fed the beast for a while on potatoes; but that was taking the bread out of his own mouth, though he supplemented it with now and then a boat-load of coarse, frost-killed grass, but the horse grew more and more gaunt and restive. His eyes glared with hunger and fury. He kicked out one side of the cowshed and snapped at Scott whenever he came near him. Want of use and food had restored him to the original savagery of his race. Hitherto Scott had never acknowledged Mrs McAlister's gift; but Sary, who had a vague idea of good manners, caught from the picture papers and occasional dime novels the tribe of Adirondack travellers strew even in such a wilderness, kept pecking at him.

"Ta'n't no more'n civil to say thank ye, to the least," she said, till Scott's temper gave way.

"Stop a-pesterin' of me! I've hed too much. I ain't a speck thankful! I'm mightily t'other thing, whatever 'tis. Write to her yourself, if you're a mind tu. You can make a better fist at it, anyways. Comes as nateral to women to lie as sap to run. I'll be etarnally blessed ef I touch paper for to do it." And he flung out of the door with a bang.

Of course Sary wrote the letter, which one balmy day electrified Harry and his mother as they sat basking in Southern sunshine:

"MIS MACALLISTUR: This is fur to say wee is reel obliged to ye fur the HOSS."

"Good gracious, mother! Did you send them a horse?" ejaculated Harry.

"Why, my dear, I wanted to show my sense of their kindness, and I could not offer these people money. I thought a horse would be so useful!"

"Useful! in the Adirondack woods!" And Harry burst into a fit of laughter that scarcely permitted his mother to go on; but at last she proceeded:

"But Scotty and me ain't ackwainted So to speak with Hoss ways; he seems kinder Hum-sick if you may say that of a Cretur. We air etarnally gratified to You for sech a Valewble Pressent, but if you was Wiling we shood Like to swapp it of in spring fur a kow, ourn Being some in years.

"yours to Command, SARY PECK."

But long before Mrs. McAlister's permission to "swap" the horse reached Scott Peck, the creature took his destiny into his own hands. Scott had gone away on a desperate errand, to fetch some sort of food for the poor creature, whose bones stared him in the face, and Sary went out one morning to give him her potato-peelings and some scraps of bread, when, suddenly, he jerked his head fiercely, snapped his halter in two, and wheeled round upon the frightened woman, rearing, snorting, and showing his long, yellow teeth. Sary fled at once and barred the door behind her; but neither she nor Scott ever saw their "gift horse" again. For aught I know he still roams the Adirondack forest, and maybe personates the ghostly and ghastly white deer of song and legend. Who can tell? But he was lifted off Scott Peck's shoulders, and all Scott said by way of epitaph on the departed, when he came home to find his white steed gone, was, "Hang presents!"

* * * * *

"Samantha Allen" will now have "a brief opportunity for remark."

Admire her graphic description of the excitement Josiah caused by voting, at a meeting of the "Jonesville Creation Searchers," for his own spouse as a delegate from Jonesville to the "Sentinel." She reports thus:

"It was a fearful time, but right where the excitement was raining most fearfully I felt a motion by the side of me, and my companion got up and stood on his feet and says, in pretty firm accents, though some sheepish:

"'I did, and there's where I stand now; I vote for Samantha!'

"And then he sot down again. Oh, the fearful excitement and confusion that rained down again! The president got up and tried to speak; the editor of the Auger talked wildly; Shakespeare Bobbet talked to himself incoherently, but

Solomon Cypher's voice drowned 'em all out, as he kep' a-smitin' his breast and a hollerin' that he wasn't goin' to be infringed upon, or come in contract with no woman!

"No female woman needn't think she was the equal of man; and I should go as a woman or stay to home. I was so almost wore out by their talk, that I spoke right out, and, says I, 'Good land! how did you s'pose I was a-goin'?'"

"The president then said that he meant, if I went I mustn't look upon things with the eye of a 'Creation Searcher' and a man (here he p'inted his forefinger right up in the air and waved it round in a real free and soarin' way), but look at things with the eye of a private investigator and a woman (here he p'inted his finger firm and stiddy right down into the wood-box and a pan of ashes). It war impressive--VERY."

MISS SLIMMENS SURPRISED.

A Terrible Accident.

BY METTA VICTORIA VICTOR.

"Dora! Dora! Dora! wake up, wake up, I say! Don't you smell something burning? Wake up, child! Don't you smell fire? Good Lord! so do I. I thought I wasn't mistaken. The room's full of smoke. Oh, dear! what'll we do? Don't stop to put on your petticoat. We'll all be burned to death. Fire! fire! fire! fire!

"Yes, there is! I don't know where! It's all over--our room's all in a blaze, and Dora won't come out till she gets her dress on. Mr. Little, you shan't go in--I'll hold you--you'll be killed just to save that chit of a girl, when--I--I--He's gone-- rushed right into the flames. Oh, my house! my furniture! all my earnings! Can't anything be done? Fire! fire! fire! Call the fire-engines! ring the dinner- bell! Be quiet! How can I be quiet? Yes, it is all in flames. I saw them myself! Where's my silver spoons? Oh, where's my teeth, and my silver soup-ladle? Let me be! I'm going out in the street before it's too late! Oh, Mr. Grayson! have you got water? have you found the place? are they bringing water?

"Did you say the fire was out? Was that you that spoke, Mr. Little? I thought you were burned up, sure; and there's Dora, too. How did they get it out? My clothes-closet was on fire, and the room, too! We would have been smothered in five minutes more if we hadn't waked up! But it's all out now, and no damage done, but my dresses destroyed and the carpet spoiled. Thank the Lord, if that's the worst! But it ain't the worst. Dora, come along this minute to my room. I don't care if it is cold, and wet, and full of smoke. Don't you see--don't you see I'm in my night-clothes? I never thought of it before. I'm ruined, ruined completely! Go to bed, gentlemen; get out of the way as quick as you can Dora, shut the door. Hand me that candle; I want to look at myself in the glass. To think that all those gentlemen should have seen me in this fix! I'd rather have perished in the flames. It's the very first night I've worn these flannel night-caps, and to be seen in 'em! Good gracious! how old I do look! Not a spear of hair on my head scarcely, and this red nightgown and old petticoat on, and my teeth in the tumbler, and the paint all washed off my face, and scarred besides! It's no use! I never, never can again make any of those men believe that I'm only twenty-five, and I felt so sure of some of them.

"Oh, Dora Adams! you needn't look pale; you've lost nothing. I'll warrant Mr. Little thought you never looked so pretty as in that ruffled gown, and your hair all down over your shoulders. He says you were fainting from the smoke when he dragged you out. You must be a little fool to be afraid to come out looking that way. They say that new boarder is a drawing-master, and I seen some of his pictures yesterday; he had some such ridiculous things. He'll caricature me for the amusement of the young men, I know. Only think how my portrait would look taken to-night! and he'll have it, I'm sure, for I noticed him looking at me--the first that reminded me of my situation after the fire was put out. Well, there's but one thing to be done, and that's to put a bold face on it. I can't sleep any more to-night; besides, the bed's wet, and it's beginning to get daylight. I'll go to work and get myself ready for breakfast, and I'll pretend to something--I don't know just what--to get myself out of this scrape, if I can....

"Good-morning, gentlemen, good-morning! We had quite a fright last night, didn't we? Dora and I came pretty near paying dear for a little frolic. You see, we were dressing up in character to amuse ourselves, and I was all fixed up for to represent an old woman, and had put on a gray wig and an old flannel gown that I found, and we'd set up pretty late, having some fun all to ourselves; and I expect Dora must have been pretty sleepy when she was putting some of the things away, and set fire to a dress in the closet without noticing it. I've lost my whole wardrobe, nigh about, by her carelessness; but it's such a mercy we wasn't burned in our bed that I don't feel to complain so much on that account. Isn't it curious how I got caught dressed up like my grandmother? We didn't suppose we were going to appear before so large an audience when we planned out our little frolic. What character did Dora assume? Really, Mr. Little, I was so scared last night that I disremember. She took off her rigging before she went to bed. Don't you think I'd personify a pretty good old woman, gentlemen--ha! ha!--for a lady of my age? What's that, Mr. Little? You wish I'd make you a present of that nightcap, to remember me by? Of course; I've no further use for it. Of course I haven't. It's one of Bridget's, that I borrowed for the occasion, and I've got to give it back to her. Have some coffee, Mr. Grayson--do! I've got cream for it this morning. Mr. Smith, help yourself to some of the beefsteak. It's a very cold morning-- fine weather out of doors. Eat all you can, all of you. Have you any profiles to take yet, Mr. Gamboge? I may make up my mind to set for mine before you leave us; I've always thought I should have it taken some time. In character? He! he! Mr. Little, you're so funny! But you'll excuse me this morning, as I had such a fright last night. I must go and take up that wet carpet."

CHAPTER V.

A BRACE OF WITTY WOMEN.

By the courtesy of Harper Brothers I am allowed to give you "Aunt Anniky's Teeth," by Sherwood Bonner. The illustrations add much, but the story is good enough without pictures.

AUNT ANNIKY'S TEETH.

BY SHERWOOD BONNER.

Aunt Anniky was an African dame, fifty years old, and of an imposing presence. As a waffle-maker she possessed a gift beyond the common, but her unapproachable talent lay in the province of nursing. She seemed born for the benefit of sick people. She should have been painted with the apple of healing in her hand. For the rest, she was a funny, illiterate old darkey, vain, affable, and neat as a pink.

On one occasion my mother had a dangerous illness. Aunt Anniky nursed her through it, giving herself no rest, night nor day, until her patient had come "back to de walks an' ways ob life," as she expressed the dear mother's recovery. My father, overjoyed and grateful, felt that we owed this result quite as much to Aunt Anniky as to our family doctor, so he announced his intention of making her a handsome present, and, like King Herod, left her free to choose what it should be. I shall never forget how Aunt Anniky looked as she stood there smiling and bowing, and bobbing the funniest little courtesies all the way down to the ground.

And you would never guess what it was the old woman asked for.

"Well, Mars' Charles," said she (she had been one of our old servants, and always called my father 'Mars' Charles'), "to tell you de livin' trufe, my soul an' body is a-yearnin' fur a han'sum chany set o' teef."

"A set of teeth!" said father, surprised enough. "And have you none left of your own?"

"I has gummed it fur a good many ye'rs," said Aunt Anniky, with a sigh; "but not wishin' ter be ongrateful ter my obligations, I owns ter havin' five nateral teef. But dey is po' sogers; dey shirks battle. One ob dem's got a little somethin' in it as lively as a speared worm, an' I tell you when anything teches it, hot or cold, it jest makes me dance! An' anudder is in my top jaw, an' ain't got no match fur it in de bottom one; an' one is broke off nearly to de root; an' de las' two is so yaller dat I's ashamed ter show 'em in company, an' so I lif's my turkey-tail ter my mouf every time I laughs or speaks."

Father turned to mother with a musing air. "The curious student of humanity," he remarked, "traces resemblances where they are not obviously conspicuous. Now, at the first blush, one would not think of any common ground of meeting for our Aunt Anniky and the Empress Josephine. Yet that fine French lady introduced the fashion of handkerchiefs by continually raising delicate lace mouchoirs to her lips to hide her bad teeth. Aunt Anniky lifts her turkey-tail! It really seems that human beings should be classed by strata, as if they were metals in the earth. Instead of dividing by nations, let us class by quality. So we might find Turk, Jew, Christian, fashionable lady and washerwoman, master and slave, hanging together like cats on a clothes-line by some connecting cord of affinity--"

"In the mean time," said my mother, mildly, "Aunt Anniky is waiting to know if she is to have her teeth."

"Oh, surely, surely!" cried father, coming out of the clouds with a start. "I am going to the village to-morrow, Anniky, in the spring wagon. I will take you with me, and we will see what the dentist can do for you."

"Bless yo' heart, Mars' Charles!" said the delighted Anniky; "you're jest as good as yo' blood and yo' name, and mo' I couldn't say."

The morrow came, and with it Aunt Anniky, gorgeously arrayed in a flaming red calico, a bandanna handkerchief, and a string of carved yellow beads that glittered on her bosom like fresh buttercups on a hill-slope.

I had petitioned to go with the party, for, as we lived on a plantation, a visit to the village was something of an event. A brisk drive soon brought us to the centre of "the Square." A glittering sign hung brazenly from a high window on its western side, bearing, in raised black letters, the name, "Doctor Alonzo Babb."

Dr. Babb was the dentist and the odd fish of our village. He beams in my memory as a big, round man, with hair and smiles all over his face, who talked incessantly, and said things to make your blood run cold.

"Do you see this ring?" he said, as he bustled about, polishing his instruments and making his preparations for the sacrifice of Aunt Anniky. He held up his right hand, on the forefinger of which glistened a ring the size of a dog-collar. "Now, what d'ye s'pose that's made of?"

"Brass," suggested father, who was funny when not philosophical.

"Brass!" cried Dr. Babb, with a withering look; "it's virgin gold, that ring is. And where d'ye s'pose I found the gold?"

My father ran his hands into his pockets in a retrospective sort of way.

"In the mouths of my patients, every grain of it," said the dentist, with a perfectly diabolical smack of the lips. "Old fillings--plugs, you know--that I saved, and had made up into this shape. Good deal of sentiment about such a ring as this."

"Sentiment of a mixed nature, I should say," murmured my father, with a grimace.

"Mixed--rather! A speck here, a speck there. Sometimes an eye, oftener a jaw, occasionally a front. More than a hundred men, I s'pose, have helped in the cause."

"Law, doctor! you beats de birds, you does," cries Aunt Anniky, whose head was as flat as the floor, where her reverence should have been. "You know dey snatches de wool from ebery bush to make deir nests."

"Lots of company for me, that ring is," said the doctor, ignoring the pertinent or impertinent interruption. "Often as I sit in the twilight, I twirl it around and around, a-thinking of the wagon-loads of food it has masticated, the blood that has flowed over it, the groans that it has cost! Now, old lady, if you will sit just here."

He motioned Aunt Anniky to the chair, into which she dropped in a limp sort of way, recovering herself immediately, however, and sitting bolt upright in a rigid attitude of defiance. Some moments of persuasion were necessary before she could be induced to lean back and allow Dr. Babb's fingers on her nose while she breathed the laughing-gas; but, once settled, the expression faded from her countenance almost as quickly as a magic-lantern picture vanishes. I watched her nervously, my attention divided between her vacant-looking face and a dreadful picture on the wall. It represented Dr. Babb himself, minus the hair, but with double the number of smiles, standing by a patient from whose mouth he had apparently just extracted a huge molar that he held triumphantly in his forceps. A gray-haired old gentleman regarded the pair with benevolent interest. The photograph was entitled, "His First Tooth."

"Attracted by that picture?" said Dr. Alonzo, affably, his fingers on Aunt

Anniky's pulse. "My par had that struck off the first time I ever got a tooth out. That's par with the gray hair and the benediction attitude. Tell you, he was proud of me! I had such an awful tussle with that tooth! Thought the old fellow's jaw was bound to break! But I got it out, and after that my par took me with him round the country--starring the provinces, you know--and I practised on the natives."

By this time Aunt Anniky was well under the influence of the gas, and in an incredibly short space of time her five teeth were out. As she came to herself I am sorry to say she was rather silly, and quite mortified me by winking at Dr. Babb in the most confidential manner, and repeating, over and over again: "Honey, yer ain't harf as smart as yer thinks yer is!"

After a few weeks of sore gums, Aunt Anniky appeared, radiant with her new teeth. The effect was certainly funny. In the first place, blackness itself was not so black as Aunt Anniky. She looked as if she had been dipped in ink and polished off with lamp-black. Her very eyes showed but the faintest rim of white. But those teeth were white enough to make up for everything. She had selected them herself, and the little ridiculous milk-white things were more fitted for the mouth of a Titania than for the great cavern in which Aunt Anniky's tongue moved and had its being. The gums above them were black, and when she spread her wide mouth in a laugh, it always reminded me of a piano-lid opening suddenly and showing all the black and white ivories at a glance. Aunt Anniky laughed a good deal, too, after getting her teeth in, and declared she had never been so happy in her life. It was observed, to her credit, that she put on no airs of pride, but was as sociable as ever, and made nothing of taking out her teeth and handing them around for inspection among her curious and admiring visitors. On that principle of human nature which glories in calling attention to the weakest part, she delighted in tough meats, stale bread, green fruits, and all other eatables that test the biting quality of the teeth. But finally destruction came upon them in a way that no one could have foreseen. Uncle Ned was an old colored man who lived alone in a cabin not very far from Aunt Anniky's, but very different from her in point of cleanliness and order. In fact, Uncle Ned's wealth, apart from a little corn crop, consisted in a lot of fine young pigs, that ran in and out of the house at all times, and were treated by their owner as tenderly as if they had been his children. One fine day the old man fell sick of a fever, and he sent in haste for Aunt Anniky to come and nurse him. He agreed to give her a pig in case she brought him through; should she fail to do so, she was to receive no pay. Well, Uncle Ned got well, and the next thing we heard was that he refused to pay the pig. My father was usually called on to settle all the disputes in the neighborhood; so one morning Anniky and Ned appeared before him, both looking very indignant.

"I'd jes' like ter tell yer, Mars' Charles," began Uncle Ned, "ob de trick dis miser'ble ole nigger played on me."

"Go on, Ned," said my father, with a resigned air.

"Well, it wuz de fift night o' de fever," said Uncle Ned, "an' I wuz a-tossin' an' a-moanin', an' old Anniky jes' lay back in her cheer an' snored as ef a dozen frogs wuz in her throat. I wuz a-perishin' an' a-burnin' wid thirst, an' I hollered to Anniky; but Lor'! I might as well 'a hollered to a tombstone! It wuz ice I wanted; an' I knowed dar wuz a glass somewhar on my table wid cracked ice in it. Lor'! Lor'! how dry I wuz! I neber longed fer whiskey in my born days ez I panted fur dat ice. It wuz powerful dark, fur de grease wuz low in de lamp, an' de wick spluttered wid a dyin' flame. But I felt aroun', feeble like an' slow, till my fingers touched a glass. I pulled it to me, an' I run my han' in an' grabbed de ice, as I s'posed, an' flung it in my mouf, an' crunched, an' crunched--"

Here there was an awful pause. Uncle Ned pointed his thumb at Anniky, looked wildly at my father, and said, in a hollow voice: "It wuz Anniky's teef!"

My father threw back his head and laughed as I had never heard him laugh. Mother from her sofa joined in. I was doubled up like a jack-knife in the corner. But as for the principals in the affair, neither of their faces moved a muscle. They saw no joke. Aunt Anniky, in a dreadful, muffled, squashy sort of voice, took up the tale:

"Nexsh ting I knowed, Marsh Sharles, somebody's sheizin' me by de head, a-jammin' it up 'gin de wall, a-jawin' at me like de Angel Gabriel at de rish ole sinners in de bad plashe--an' dar wash ole Ned a-spittin' like a black cat, an' a-howlin' so dreadful dat I tought he wash de debil; an' when I got de light, dar wash my beautiful chany teef a-flung aroun', like scattered seed-corn, on de flo', an' Ned a-swarin' he'd have de law o' me."

"An' arter all dat," broke in Uncle Ned, "she pretends to lay a claim fur my pig. But I says no, sir; I don't pay nobody nothin' who's played me a trick like dat."

"Trick!" said Aunt Anniky, scornfully, "whar's de trick? Tink I wanted yer ter eat my teef? An' furder-mo', Marsh Sharles, dar's jes' dis about it: when dat night set in dar warn't no mo' hope fur old Ned dan fur a foundered sheep. Laws-a-massy! dat's why I went ter sleep. I wanted ter hev strengt' ter put on his burial clo'es in de mornin'. But don' yer see, Marsh Sharles, dat when he got so mad it brought on a sweat dat broke de fever! It saved him! But, fur all dat, arter munchin' an' manglin' my chany teef, he has de imperdence ob tryin' to 'prive me ob de pig I honestly 'arned."

It was a hard case. Uncle Ned sat there a very image of injured dignity, while Aunt Anniky bound a red handkerchief around her mouth and fanned herself with her turkey-tail.

"I am sure I don't know how to settle the matter," said father, helplessly. "Ned, I don't see but that you'll have to pay up."

"Neber, Mars' Charles, neber."

"Well, suppose you get married?" suggested father, brilliantly. "That will unite your interests, you know."

Aunt Anniky tossed her head. Uncle Ned was old, wizened, wrinkled as a raisin, but he eyed Anniky over with a supercilious gaze, and said with dignity: "Ef I wanted ter marry, I could git a likely young gal."

All the four points of Anniky's turban shook with indignation. "Pay me fur dem chany teef!" she hissed.

Some visitors interrupted the dispute at this time, and the two old darkies went away.

A week later Uncle Ned appeared with rather a sheepish look.

"Well, Mars' Charles," he said, "I's about concluded dat I'll marry Anniky."

"Ah! is that so?"

"'Pears like it's de onliest way I kin save my pigs," said Uncle Ned, with a sigh. "When she's married she boun' ter 'bey me. Women 'bey your husbands; dat's what de good Book says."

"Yes, she will bay you, I don't doubt," said my father, making a pun that Uncle Ned could not appreciate.

"An' ef ever she opens her jaw ter me 'bout dem ar teef," he went on, "I'll mash her."

Uncle Ned tottered on his legs like an unscrewed fruit-stand, and I had my own opinion as to his "mashing" Aunt Anniky. This opinion was confirmed the next day when father offered her his congratulations. "You are old enough to know your own mind," he remarked.

"I's ole, maybe," said Anniky, "but so is a oak-tree, an' it's vigorous, I reckon. I's a purty vigorous sort o' growth myself, an' I reckon I'll have my own way with Ned. I'm gwine ter fatten dem pigs o' hisn, an' you see ef I don't sell 'em nex' Christmas fur money 'nouf ter git a new string o' chany teef."

"Look here, Anniky," said father, with a burst of generosity, "you and Ned will quarrel about those teeth till the day of doom, so I will make you a wedding present of another set, that you may begin married life in harmony."

Aunt Anniky expressed her gratitude. "An' dis time," she said, with sudden fury, "I sleeps wid 'em in."

The teeth were presented, and the wedding preparations began. The expectant bride went over to Ned's cabin and gave it such a clearing up as it had never had. But Ned did not seem happy. He devoted himself entirely to his pigs, and wandered about looking more wizened every day. Finally he came to our gate and beckoned to me mysteriously.

"Come over to my house, honey," he whispered, "an' bring a pen an' ink an' a piece o' paper wid yer. I wants yer ter write me a letter."

I ran into the house for my little writing-desk, and followed Uncle Ned to his cabin.

"Now, honey," he said, after barring the door carefully, "don't you ax me no questions, but jes' put down de words dat comes out o' my mouf on dat ar paper."

"Very well, Uncle Ned, go on."

"Anniky Hobbleston," he began, "dat weddin' ain't a-gwine ter come off. You cleans up too much ter suit me. I ain't used ter so much water splashin' aroun'. Dirt is warmin'. 'Spec I'd freeze dis winter if you wuz here. An' you got too much tongue. Besides, I's got anudder wife over in Tipper. An' I ain't a-gwine ter marry. As fur havin' de law, I's a leavin' dese parts, an' I takes der pigs wid me. Yer can't fin' dem, an' yer can't fin' me. Fur I ain't a-gwine ter marry. I wuz born a bachelor, an' a bachelor will I represent myself befo' de judgment-seat. If you gives yer promise ter say no mo' 'bout dis marryin' business, p'r'aps I'll come back some day. So no mo' at present, from your humble worshipper,

"NED CUDDY."

"Isn't that last part rather inconsistent?" said I, greatly amused.

"Yes, honey, if yer says so; an' it's kind o' soothin' to de feelin's of a woman, yer know."

I wrote it all down and read it aloud to Uncle Ned.

"Now, my chile," he said, "I'm a-gwine ter git on my mule as soon as der moon rises, an' drive my pigs ter Col' Water Gap, whar I'll stay an' fish. Soon as I am well gone, you take dis letter ter Anniky; but min', don't tell whar I's gone. An' if she takes it all right, an' promises ter let me alone, you write me a letter, an' I'll git de fust Methodis' preacher I run across in der woods ter read it ter me. Den, ef it's all right, I'll come back an' weed yer flower-garden fur yer as purty as preachin'."

I agreed to do all uncle Ned asked, and we parted like conspirators. The next morning Uncle Ned was missing, and, after waiting a reasonable time I explained the matter to my parents, and went over with his letter to Aunt Anniky.

"Powers above!" was her only comment as I got through the remarkable epistle. Then, after a pause to collect her thoughts, she seized me by the shoulder, saying: "Run to yo' pappy, honey, quick, an' ax him ef he's gwine ter stick ter his bargain 'bout de teef. Yer know he pintedly said dey wuz a weddin' gif'."

Of course my father sent word that she must keep the teeth, and my mother added a message of sympathy, with a present of a pocket-handkerchief to dry Aunt Anniky's tears.

"But it's all right," said that sensible old soul, opening her piano-lid with a cheerful laugh. "Bless you, chile, it wuz de teef I wanted, not de man! An', honey, you jes' sen' word to dat shif'less old nigger, ef you know whar he's gone, to come back home and git his crap in de groun'; an', as fur as I'm consarned, yer jes' let him know dat I wouldn't pick him up wid a ten-foot pole, not ef he wuz to beg me on his knees till de millennial day."--From "Dialect Tales," published in 1883 by Harper Brothers.

* * * * *

It is not easy to tell what satire is, or where it originated. "In Eden," says Dryden, "the husband and wife excused themselves by laying the blame on each other, and gave a beginning to those conjugal dialogues in prose which poets have perfected in verse." Whatever it may be, we know it when it cuts us, and Sherwood Bonner's hit on the Radical Club of Boston was almost inexcusable.

She was admitted as a guest, and her subsequent ridicule was a violation of all good breeding. But like so many wicked things it is captivating, and while you are shocked, you laugh. While I hold up both hands in horror, I intend to give you an idea of it; leaving out the most personal verses.

THE RADICAL CLUB.

BY SHERWOOD BONNER.

Dear friends, I crave attention to some facts that I shall mention About a Club called "Radical," you haven't heard before; Got up to teach the nation was this new light federation, To teach the nation how to think, to live, and to adore; To teach it of the heights and depths that all men should explore; Only this and nothing more.

It is not my inclination, in this brief communication, To produce a false impression--which I greatly would deplore-- But a few remarks I'm makin' on some notes a chiel's been takin,' And, if I'm not mistaken, they'll make your soul upsoar, As you bend your eyes with eagerness to scan these verses o'er; Truly this and something more.

And first, dear friends, the fact is, I'm sadly out of practice, And may fail in doing justice to this literary bore; But when I do begin it, I don't think 'twill take a minute To prove there's nothing in it (as you've doubtless heard before), But a free religious wrangling club--of this I'm very sure-- Only this and nothing more!

'Twas a very cordial greeting, one bright morning of their meeting; Such eager salutations were never heard before. After due deliberation on the importance of the occasion, To begin the organization, Mr. Pompous took the floor With an air quite self-complacent, strutted up and took the floor, As he'd often done before!

With an air of condescension he bespoke their close attention To an essay from a Wiseman versed in theologic lore; He himself had had the pleasure of a short glance at the treasure, And in no stinted measure said we had a treat in store; Then he waved his hand to Wiseman and resigned to him the floor; Only this and nothing more.

Quick and nervous, short and wiry, with a look profound, yet fiery, Mr. Wiseman now stepped forward and eyed us darkly o'er, Then an arm-chair, quaint and olden, gay with colors green and golden, By the pretty hostess rolled in from its place behind the door, Was offered to the reader, in the centre of the floor, And he took the chair be sure.

Then with arguments elastic, and a voice and eye sarcastic, Mr. Wiseman into flinders the Holy Bible tore; And he proved beyond all question that the God of Moses' mention Was a fraudulent invention of some Hebrews, three or four, And the Son of God's ascension an imaginary soar! Only this and nothing more.

Each member then admitted that his part was well acquitted, For his strong, impassioned reasoning had touched them to the core; He felt sure, as he surveyed them through his specs, that he had "played" them, And was proud that he had made them all astonished by his lore; Not a continental cared he for the fruits such lessons bore, So he bowed and left the floor.

Then a Colonel, cold and smiling, with a stately air beguiling, Who punctuates his paragraphs on Newport's sounding shore, Said his friend was wise and witty, and yet it seemed a pity To destroy in this old city the belief it had before In the ancient superstitions of the days of yore. This he said, and something more.

Orthodoxy, he lamented, thought the Christian world demented, Yet still he felt a rev'rence as he read the Bible o'er, And he thought the modern preacher, though a poor stick for a teacher, Or a broken reed, like Beecher, ought to have his claims looked o'er, And the "tyranny of science" was indeed, he felt quite sure, Our danger more and more.

His remarks our pulses quicken, when a British Lion, stricken With his wondrous self-importance--he knew everything and more-- Said he loathed such moderation; and he made his declaration That, in spite of all creation, he found no God to adore; And his voice was like the ocean as its surges loudly roar; Only this and nothing more.

* * * * *

But the interest now grew lukewarm, for an ancient Concord book-worm With authoritative tramping, forward came and took the floor, And in Orphic mysticisms talked of life and light and prisms, And the Infinite baptisms on a transcendental shore, And the concrete metaphysic, till we yawned in anguish sore; But still he kept the floor.

Then uprose a kindred spirit almost ready to inherit The rare and radiant Aiden that he begged us to adore; His smile was beaming brightly, and his soft hair floated whitely Round a face as fair and sightly as a pious priest's of yore; And we forgave the arguments worn out years before, For we loved this saintly bore.

* * * * *

Then a lively little charmer, noted as a dress reformer, Because that mystic garment, chemiloon, she wore, Said she had no "views" of Jesus, and therefore would not tease us, But that she thought 'twould please us to look her figure o'er, For she wore no bustles anywhere, and corsets, she felt sure, Should squeeze her nevermore.

This pretty little pigeon said of course the true religion Demanded ease of body before the mind could soar; But that no emancipation could come unto our nation Until the aggregation of the clothes that women wore Were suspended from the shoulders, and smooth with many a gore, Plain behind and plain before!

Her remarks were full of reason, but a little out of season, And the proper tone of talking Mr. Fairman did restore, When he sneered at priests and preaching, and indorsed the Index teaching, And with philanthropic screeching, said he sought for evermore The light of sense and freedom into darkened minds to pour; Truly this, but something more!

Then with eyes as bright as Phoebus, and hair dark as Erebus, A maid with stunning eye-glass next appeared upon the floor; In her aspect she looked regal, though her words were few and feeble, But she vowed his logic legal and as pure as golden ore, And indorsed the Index editor in every word he swore, And then--said nothing more.

Then a tall and red-faced member, large and loose and somewhat limber (And though his creed was shaky, he the name of Bishop bore), Said that if he lived forever, he should forget, ah! never, The Radicals so clever, in Boston by the shore; But a bad gold in his 'ead bust stop his saying bore, And we all cried encore.

* * * * *

Then a rarely gifted mortal, to whom the triple portal Of Music, Art, and Poesy had opened years before, With a look of sombre feeling, depths within his soul revealing, Leaving room for no appealing, he decided o'er and o'er The old, old vexing questions of the why and the wherefore, And taught us-- nothing more.

There are others I could mention who took part in this contention, And at first 'twas my intention, but at present I forbear; There's young Look-sharp, and Wriggle, who would make an angel giggle, And a young conceited Zeigel, who was seated near the door; If you could only see them, you'd laugh till you were sore, And then you'd laugh some more.

But, dear friends, I now must close, of these Radicals dispose, For I am sad and weary as I view their folly o'er; In their wild Utopian dreaming, and impracticable scheming For a sinful world's redeeming, common sense flies out the door, And the long-drawn dissertations come to--words and nothing more; Only words, and nothing more.

* * * * *

Mary Clemmer Hudson has spoken of Phoebe Cary as "the wittiest woman in America." But she truly adds:

"A flash of wit, like a flash of lightning, can only be remembered, it cannot be reproduced. Its very marvel lies in its spontaneity and evanescence; its power is in being struck from the present. Divorced from that, the keenest representation of it seems cold and dead. We read over the few remaining sentences which attempt to embody the repartees and bon mots of the most famous wits of society, such as Beau Nash, Beau Brummel, Madame du Deffand, and Lady Mary Montagu; we wonder at the poverty of these memorials of their fame. Thus it must be with Phoebe Cary. Her most brilliant sallies were perfectly unpremeditated, and by herself never repeated or remembered. When she was in her best moods they came like flashes of heat lightning, like a rush of meteors, so suddenly and constantly you were dazzled while you were delighted, and afterward found it difficult to single out any distinct flash or separate meteor from the multitude.... This most wonderful of her gifts can only be represented by a few stray sentences gleaned here and there from the faithful memories of loving friends....

"One tells how, at a little party, where fun rose to a great height, one quiet person was suddenly attacked by a gay lady with the question: 'Why don't you laugh? You sit there just like a post!'

"'There! she called you a post; why don't you rail at her?' was Phoebe's quick exclamation.

"Mr. Barnum mentioned to her that the skeleton man and the fat woman then on exhibition in his 'greatest show on earth' were married.

"'I suppose they loved through thick and thin,' was her comment.

"'On one occasion, when Phoebe was at the Museum looking about at the curiosities,' says Mr. Barnum, 'I preceded her and had passed down a couple of steps. She, intently watching a big anaconda in a case at the top of the stairs, walked off, not noticing them, and fell. I was just in time to catch her in my arms and save her from a good bruising'.

"'I am more lucky than that first woman was who fell through the influence of the serpent,' said Phoebe, as she recovered herself.

"And when asked by some one at a dinner-party what brand of champagne they kept, she replied: 'Oh, we drink Heidsieck, but we keep Mum.'

"Again, a certain well-known actor, then recently deceased, and more conspicuous for his professional skill than for his private virtues, was discussed. 'We shall never,' remarked some one, 'see ---- again.'

"'No,' quietly responded Phoebe, 'not unless we go to the pit.'"

These stray shots may not fairly represent Miss Cary's brilliancy, but we are grateful for what has been preserved, meagre as it would seem to those who had the privilege of knowing her intimately and enjoying those Sunday evening receptions, where, unrestrained and happy, every one was at his best.

Her verses on the subject of Woman's Rights, as discussed in masculine fashion, with masculine logic, by Chanticleer Dorking, are capital, and her parodies, shockingly literal, have been widely copied. Enjoy these as given in her life, written by Mary Clemmer.

CHAPTER VI.

GINGER-SNAPS.

I will now offer you some good things of various degrees of humor. I do not feel it necessary to impress their merits upon you, for they speak for themselves Here is a quaint bit of satire from a bright Boston woman, which those on her side of the vexed Indian question will enjoy:

THE INDIAN AGENT.

BY LOUISA HALL.

He was a long, lean man, with a sad expression, as if weighed down by pity for poor humanity. His heart was evidently a great many sizes too large for him. He yearned to enfold all tribes and conditions of men in his encircling arms. He surveyed his audience with such affectionate interest that he seemed to look into the very depths of their pockets.

A few resolute men buttoned their coats, but the majority knew that this artifice would not save them, and they rather enjoyed it as a species of harmless dissipation. They liked to be talked into a state of exhilaration which obliged them to give without thinking much about it, and they felt very good and benevolent afterward. So they cheered the agent enthusiastically, as a signal for him to begin, and he came forward bowing, while the three red brothers who accompanied him remained seated on the platform. He appeared to smile on every one present as he said:

"Friends and Fellow-Citizens, I have the honor to introduce to you these chiefs of the Laughing Dog Nation. Twenty-five years ago this tribe was one of the fiercest on our Western plains. Snarling Bear, the most noted chief of his tribe, was a great warrior. Fifty scalps adorned his wigwam. Some of them had once belonged to his best friends. He was murdered while in the prime of life by a white man whose wife he had accidentally shot at the door of her cabin. He was one of the first to welcome the white men and adopt the improvements they brought with them. When he became sufficiently civilized to understand that polygamy was unlawful, he separated from his oldest wife. Her scalp was carefully preserved among those of the great warriors he had conquered. His son, Flying Deer, who is with us to-day, will address you in his own language, which I shall interpret for you. The last twenty years have made a great change in their condition. These men are not savages, but educated gentlemen. They are all graduates of Tomahawk College, at Bloody Mountain, near the Gray Wolf country. They are chiefs of their tribes, each one holding a position equal to the Governor of our own State. Their influence at the West is great. Last year they sent a small party of missionaries to the highlands of the Wolf country, where the women and children pasture the ponies during the dry season. Not one of these noble men ever returned. Unfortunately for the success of this mission, the Gray Wolf warriors were at home. The medicine man's dreams had been unfavorable, and they dared not set out on their annual hunt. This year they will send a larger party well armed.

"These devoted men have left their Western homes and come here to assure you of their confidence in your affection, and the love and gratitude they feel toward you. They come to ask for churches and schools, that their children may grow up like yours. But these things require money. On account of the great scarcity of stone in the Rocky Mountains, and the necessity of preserving standing timber for the Indian hunting-grounds, all building materials for churches and school-houses must be carried from the East at great expense. The door-steps of the third orthodox Kickapoo church cost one hundred and fifty dollars. But it is money well invested. The gradual decrease of crime at the West has convinced the most sceptical that a great work can be done among these people. The number of murders committed in this country last year was one hundred and twenty-five; this year only one hundred and twenty-three.

"Although a great deal has been done for these people, you will be surprised to learn how much remains to be done. I need not tell you that every dollar intrusted to me will be spent, and I hope you will live to see the result of your generosity.

"I wish to build at least fifteen churches and school-houses before the cold weather sets in. The cost of building has been greatly lessened by employing native workmen, who are capable of designing and erecting simple edifices. The pulpits will be supplied by native preachers, and the expense of light and heat will be paid by the congregation.

"We have at least twenty-five well-qualified native teachers, who will require no salary beyond the necessary expense of food and clothing.

"A few boarding-houses must be built and tastefully furnished. We have a large number of Laughing Dog widows, who would gladly take charge of such establishments.

"The native committee will make a careful selection of such matrons as are most capable of guiding and encouraging young people.

"All money for the benefit of these people has been used with the strictest economy; and will be while I retain the agency. I have secured a slender provision for my declining years, and shall return to spend my days with my adopted people.

"But I will let these men who once owned this great country speak for themselves. Flying Deer, who will now address you, is about forty years of age. He lives with his wife and ten children near the agency, at a place called Humanketchet."

Flying Deer came forward and spoke very distinctly, though rapidly.

"O hoo bree-gutchee, gumme maw choo kibbe showain nemeshin. Dawmasse choochugah goo waugh; kawboo. Nokka brewis goo, honowin nudwag moonoo shugh kawmun menjeis. Babas kwasind waugh muskoday, wawa gessonwon goo. Nahna naskeen oza yenadisse mayben mudjo, kenemoosha. Wawconassee nushka kahgagoo, jossahut, wabenas ogu winemon jabs. Ahmuck wana wayroossen chooponnuk segwan maysen. Opeechee annewayman, kewadoda shenghen kad goo tagamengow."

"He says, my friends, that he has always loved and trusted the white people.

He says that since he has seen the great cities and towns of the East, he loves his white brothers more than before. His red brothers, White Crow and the Rock on End, wish him to say that they also love you. He says the savage Gray Wolf tribe threaten to shoot and scalp them if they continue friendly to the whites. He asks for powder, guns, and ponies, that they may defend themselves from their enemies. He wants to convince you that they are rapidly becoming a civilized nation. The assistance you are about to give will only be required for a short time. They will soon become self-supporting, and relieve the Government of a heavy tax. They thank you for the kindness you have shown, and for the generous collection which will now be taken up.

"Will some friend close the doors while we give every one an opportunity to contribute to this good cause? Remember that he who shutteth up his ears to the cry of the poor, he shall also cry himself and shall not be heard. Those who prefer can leave a check with Deacon Meekham at the door, or with me at the hotel. These substantial tokens of your regard will cause the wilderness to blossom as the rose.

"In the name of our red brethren, let me again thank you."

* * * * *

If one inclines to Irish fun, try this burlesque from Mrs. Lippincott.

MISTRESS O'RAFFERTY ON THE WOMAN QUESTION.

BY GRACE GREENWOOD.

No! I wouldn't demane myself, Bridget, Like you, in disputin' with men-- Would I fly in the face of the blissed Apostles, an' Father Maginn?

It isn't the talent I'm wantin'-- Sure my father, ould Michael McCrary, Made a beautiful last spache and confession When they hanged him in ould Tipperary.

So, Bridget Muldoon, howld yer talkin' About Womins' Rights, and all that! Sure all the rights I want is the one right, To be a good helpmate to Pat;

For he's a good husband--and niver Lays on me the weight of his hand Except when he's far gone in liquor, And I nag him, you'll plase understand.

Thrue for ye, I've one eye in mournin', That's becaze I disputed his right, To tak' and spind all my week's earnin's At Tim Mulligan's wake, Sunday night.

But it's sildom when I've done a washin', He'll ask for more'n half of the pay; An' he'll toss me my share, wid a smile, dear, That's like a swate mornin' in May!

Now where, if I rin to convintions, Will be Patrick's home-comforts and joys? Who'll clane up his broghans for Sunday, Or patch up his ould corduroys.

If we tak' to the polls, night and mornin', Our dilicate charms will all flee-- The dew will be brushed from the rose, dear, The down from the pache-- don't you see?

We'll soon tak' to shillalahs and shindies Whin we get to be sovereign electors, And turn all our husbands' hearts from us, Thin what will we do for protectors?

We'll have to be crowners an' judges, An' such like ould malefactors, Or they'll make Common Councilmin of us; Thin where will be our char-acters?

Oh, Bridget, God save us from votin'! For sure as the blissed sun rolls, We'll land in the State House or Congress, Thin what will become of our sowls?

* * * * *

Or the triumphs of a quack, by Miss Amanda T. Jones.

DOCHTHER O'FLANNIGAN AND HIS WONDHERFUL CURES.

I.

I'm Barney O'Flannigan, lately from Cork; I've crossed the big watther as bould as a shtork. 'Tis a dochther I am and well versed in the thrade; I can mix yez a powdher as good as is made. Have yez pains in yer bones or a throublesome ache In yer jints afther dancin' a jig at a wake? Have yez caught a black eye from some blundhering whack? Have yez vertebral twists in the sphine av yer back? Whin ye're walkin' the shtrates are yez likely to fall? Don't whiskey sit well on yer shtomick at all? Sure 'tis botherin' nonsinse to sit down and wape Whin a bit av a powdher ull put yez to shlape. Shtate yer symptoms, me darlins, and niver yez doubt But as sure as a gun I can shtraighten yez out! Thin don't yez be gravin' no more; Arrah! quit all yer sighin' forlorn; Here's Barney O'Flannigan right to the fore, And bedad! he's a gintleman born!

II.

Coom thin, ye poor craytures and don't yez be scairt! Have yez batin' and lumberin' thumps at the hairt, Wid ossification, and acceleration, Wid fatty accretion and bad vellication, Wid liver inflation and hapitization, Wid lung inflammation and brain-adumbration, Wid black aruptation and schirrhous formation, Wid nerve irritation and paralyzation, Wid extravasation and acrid sacration, Wid great jactitation and exacerbation, Wid shtrong palpitation and wake circulation, Wid quare titillation and cowld perspiration? Be the powers! but I'll bring all yer woes to complation, Onless yer in love--thin yer past all salvation! Coom, don't yez be gravin' no more! Be quit wid yer sighin' forlorn; Here's the man all yer haling potations to pour, And ye'll prove him a gintleman born

III.

Sure, me frinds, 'tis the wondherful luck I have had In the thratement av sickness no matther how bad. All the hundhreds I've cured 'tis not aisy to shpake, And if any sowl dies, faith I'm in at the wake; There was Misthriss O'Toole was tuck down mighty quare, That wild there was niver a one dared to lave her; And phat was the matther? Ye'll like for to hare; 'Twas the double quotidian humerous faver. Well, I tuck out me lancet and pricked at a vein, (Och, murther! but didn't she howl at the pain!) Six quarts, not a dhrap less I drew widout sham, And troth she shtopped howlin', and lay like a lamb. Thin for fare sich a method av thratement was risky, I hasthened to fill up the void wid ould whiskey. Och! niver be gravin' no more! Phat use av yer sighin' forlorn? Me patients are proud av me midical lore-- They'll shware I'm a gintleman born.

IV.

Well, Misthriss O'Toole was tuck betther at once, For she riz up in bed and cried: "Paddy, ye dunce! Give the dochther a dhram." So I sat at me aise A-brewin' the punch jist as fine as ye plaze. Thin I lift a prascription all written down nate Wid ametics and diaphoretics complate; Wid anti-shpasmodics to kape her so quiet, And a toddy so shtiff that ye'd all like to thry it. So Paddy O'Toole mixed 'em well in a cup-- All barrin' the toddy, and that be dhrunk up; For he shwore 'twas a shame sich good brandy to waste On a double quotidian faverish taste; And troth we agrade it was not bad to take, Whin we dhrank that same toddy nixt night--at the wake! Arrah! don't yez be gravin' no more, Wid yer moanin' and sighin' forlorn; Here's Barney O'Flannigan thrue to the core Av the hairt of a gintleman born!

V.

There was Michael McDonegan down wid a fit Caught av dhrinkin' cowld watther--whin tipsy--a bit. 'Twould have done yer hairt good to have heard him cry out For a cup of potheen or a tankard av shtout, Or a wee dhrap av whiskey, new out av the shtill;-- And the shnakes that he saw--troth 'twas jist fit to kill! It was Mania Pototororum, bedad! Holy Mither av Moses! the divils he had! Thin to scare 'em away we surronded his bed, Clapt on forty laches and blisthered his head, Bate all the tin pans and set up sich a howl, That the last fiery divil ran off, be me sowl! And we writ on his tombsthone, "He died av a shpell Caught av dhrinkin' cowld watther shtraight out av a well." Now don't yez be gravin' no more, Surrinder yer sighin' forlorn! 'Twill be fine whin ye cross to the Stygian shore, To be sint by a gintleman born.

VI.

There was swate Ellen Mulligan, sazed wid a cough, And ivery one said it would carry her off. "Whisht," says I, "thrust to me, now, and don't yez go crazy; If the girlie must die, sure I'll make her die aisy!" So I sairched through me books for the thrue diathesis Of morbus dyscrasia tuburculous phthasis; And I boulsthered her up wid the shtrongest av tonics. Wid iron and copper and hosts av carbonics; Wid whiskey served shtraight in the finest av shtyle, And I grased all her inside wid cod-liver ile! And says she (whin she died),

"Och, dochther, me honey, 'Tis you as can give us the worth av our money; And begorra, I'll shpake to the divil this day Not to kape yez a-waitin' too long for yer pay." So don't yez be gravin' no more! To the dogs wid yer sighin' forlorn! Here's dhrugs be the handful and pills be the score, And to dale thim a gintleman born.

VII.

There was Teddy Maloney who bled at the nose Afther blowin' the fife; and mayhap ye'd suppose 'Twas no matther at all; but the books all agrade 'Twas a serious visceral throuble indade; Wid the blood swimmin' roond in a circle elliptic, The Schneidarian membrane was wantin' a shtyptic; The anterior nares were nadin' a plug, And Teddy himself was in nade av a jug. Thin I rowled out a big pill av sugar av lead, And I dosed him, and shtood him up firm on his head, And says I: "Now, me lad, don't be atin' yer lingth, But dhrink all ye plaze, jist to kape up yer shtringth." Faith! His widdy's a jewel! But whisht! don't ye shpake! She'll be Misthriss O'Flannigan airly nixt wake. Coom, don't yez be gravin' no more! Shmall use av yer sighin' forlorn; For yer widdies, belike, whin their mournin' is o'er, May marry some gintleman born.

VIII.

Ould Biddy O'Cardigan lived all alone, And she felt mighty nate wid a house av her own-- Shwate-smellin' and houlsome, swaped clane wid a rake, Wid two or thray pigs jist for company's sake. Well, phat should she get but the malady vile Av cholera-phobia-vomitus-bile! And she sint straight for me: "Dochther Barney, me lad," Says she, "I'm in nade av assistance, bedad! Have yez niver a powdher or bit av a pill? Me shtomick's a rowlin'; jist make it kape shtill!" "I'm the boy can do that," says I; "hould on a minit, Here's me midicine-chist wid me calomel in it, And I'll make yez a bowle full av rid pipper tay So shtrong ye'll be thinkin' the divil's to pay," Now don't yez be gravin' no more! Be quit wid yer sighin' forlorn, Wid shtrychnine and vitriol and opium galore, Behould me--a gintleman born.

IX.

Wid a gallon av rum thin a flip I created, Shwate, wid musthard and shpice; and the poker I hated As rid as a guinea jist out av the mint-- And into her shtomick, begorra, it wint! Och, niver belave me, but didn't she roar! I'd have kaped her alive wid a quart or two more; And the thray little pigs in that house av her own Wouldn't now be a-shtarvin' and shqualin' alone. And that gossoon, her boy--the shpalpeen altogither!-- Would niver have shworn that I murdhered his mither. Troth, for sayin' that same, but I served him a thrick, Whin I met him by chance wid a bit av a shtick. Faith, I dochthered him well till the cure I complated, And, be jabers! there's one man alive that I thrated! So don't yez be gravin' no more; To the dogs wid yez sighin' forlorn! Arrah! knock whin ye're sick at O'Flannigan's door, And die for a gintleman born!

--Scribner's Magazine. 1880.

* * * * *

Or, if one prefers to laugh at the experience of a "culled" brother, what can be found more irresistible than this?

THE OLD-TIME RELIGION.

BY JULIA PICKERING.

Brother Simon. I say, Brover Horace, I hearn you give Meriky de terriblest beating las' nite. What you and she hab a fallin'-out about?

Brother Horace. Well, Brover Simon, you knows yourself I never has no dejection to splanifying how I rules my folks at home, and 'stablishes order dar when it's p'intedly needed; and 'fore gracious! I leab you to say dis time ef 'twant needed, and dat pow'ful bad.

You see, I'se allers been a plain, straight-sided nigger, an' hain't never had no use for new fandangles, let it be what it mout; 'ligion, polytix, bisness-- don't ker what. Ole Horace say: "De ole way am de bes' way, an' you niggers dat's all runnin' teetotleum crazy 'bout ebery new gimerack dat's started, better jes' stay whar you is and let them things alone." But dey won't do it; no 'mount of preaching won't sarve um. And dat is jes' at this partickeler pint dat Meriky got dat dressin'. She done been off to Richmun town, a-livin' in sarvice dar dis las' winter, and Saturday a week ago she camed home ter make a visit. Course we war all glad to see our darter. But you b'l'eve dat gal hadn't turned stark bodily naked fool? Yes, sir; she wa'n't no more like de Meriky dat went away jes' a few munts ago dan chalk's like cheese. Dar she come in wid her close pinned tight enuff to hinder her from squattin', an' her ha'r a-danglin' right in her eyes, jes' for all de worl' like a ram a-looking fru a brush-pile, and you think dat nigger hain't forgot how to talk! She jes' rolled up her eyes ebery oder word, and fanned and talked like she 'spected to die de nex' breff. She'd toss dat mush-head ob hern and talk proper as two dixunarys. 'Stead ob she call-in' ob me "daddy" and her mudder "mammy," she say: "Par and mar, how can you bear to live in sech a one-hoss town as this? Oh! I think I should die." And right about dar she hab all de actions ob an' old drake in a thunder-storm. I jes' stared at dat gal tell I make her out, an' says I to myself: "It's got to come;" but I don't say nothin' to nobody 'bout it--all de same I knowed it had to come fus' as las'. Well, I jes' let her hab more rope, as de sayin' is, tell she got whar I 'cluded war 'bout de end ob her tedder. Dat was on last Sunday mornin', when she went to meetin' in sich a rig, a-puttin' on airs, tell she couldn't keep a straight track. When she camed home she brung kumpny wid her, and, ob course, I couldn't do nuthin' then; but I jes' kept my ears open, an' ef dat gal didn't disquollify me dat day, you ken hab my hat. Bimeby dey all gits to talkin' 'bout 'ligion and de churches, and den one young buck he step up, an' says he: "Miss Meriky, give us your 'pinion 'bout de matter." Wid dat she flung up her head proud as de Queen Victory, an' says she: "I takes no intelligence in sich matters; dey is all too common for me. Baptisses is a foot or two below my grade. I 'tends de 'Pisclopian Church whar I resides, an' 'specs to jine dat one de nex' anniversary ob de bishop. Oh! dey does eberything so lovely, and in so much style. I declar' nobody but common folks in de city goes to de Babtiss Church. It made me sick 't my stomuck to see so much shoutin' and groanin' dis mornin'; 'tis so ungenteel wid us to make so much sarcumlocutions in meetin'." And thar she went a-giratin' 'bout de preacher a-comin' out in a white shirt, and den a-runnin' back and gittin' on a black one, and de people a-jumpin' up and a-jawin' ob de preacher outen a book, and a-bowin' ob deir heads, and a-saying long rigmaroles o' stuff, tell my head fairly buzzed, and were dat mad at de gal I jes' couldn't see nuffin' in dat room. Well, I jes' waited tell the kumpny riz to go, and den I steps up, and says I: "Young folks, you needn't let what Meriky told you 'bout dat church put no change inter you. She's sorter out ob her right mine now, but de nex' time you comes she'll be all right on dat and seberal oder subjicks;" and den dey stared at Meriky mighty hard and goed away.

Well, I jes' walks up to her, and I says: "Darter," says I, "what chu'ch are dat you say you gwine to jine?" And says she, very prompt like: "De 'Pisclopian, pa." And says I: "Meriky, I'se mighty consarned 'bout you, kase I knows your mine ain't right, and I shall jes' hab to bring you roun' de shortest way possible." So I retch me a fine bunch of hick'ries I done prepared for dat 'casion. And den she jumped up, and says she: "What make you think I loss my senses?" "Bekase, darter, you done forgot how to walk and to talk, and dem is sure signs." And wid dat I jes' let in on her tell I 'stonished her 'siderably. 'Fore I were done wid her she got ober dem dying a'rs, and jumped as high as a hopper-grass. Bimeby she 'gins to holler: "Oh, Lordy, daddy! daddy! don't give me no more."

And says I: "You're improvin', dat's a fac'; done got your natural voice back. What chu'ch does you 'long to, Meriky?" And says she, a-cryin': "I don't 'long to none, par."

Well, I gib her anodder leetle tetch, and says I: "What chu'ch does you 'long to, darter?" And says she, all choked like: "I doesn't 'long to none."

Den I jes' make dem hick'ries ring for 'bout five minutes, and den I say: "What chu'ch you 'longs to now, Meriky?" And says she, fairly shoutin': "Baptiss; I'se a deep-water Baptiss." "Berry good," says I. "You don't 'spect to hab your name tuck offen dem chu'ch books?" And says she: "No, sar; I allus did despise dem stuck-up 'Pisclopians; dey ain't got no 'ligion nohow."

Brover Simon, you never see a gal so holpen by a good genteel thrashin' in all your days. I boun' she won't neber stick her nose in dem new-fandangle chu'ches no more. Why, she jes' walks as straight dis morning, and looks as peart as a sunflower. I'll lay a tenpence she'll be a-singin' before night dat good ole hyme she usened to be so fond ob. You knows, Brover Simon, how de words run:

"Baptis, Baptis is my name, My name is written on high; 'Spects to lib and die de same, My name is written on high."

Brother Simon. Yes, dat she will, I be boun'; ef I does say it, Brover Horace, you beats any man on church guberment an' family displanement ob anybody I ever has seen.

Brother Horace. Well, Brover, I does my bes'. You mus' pray for me, so dat my han's may be strengthened. Dey feels mighty weak after dat conversion I give dat Meriky las' night.--Scribner's Monthly, Bric-?Brac, 1876.

* * * * *

If it is unadulterated consolation that you need, try

AUNTY DOLEFUL'S VISIT.

BY MARY KYLE DALLAS.

How do you do, Cornelia? I heard you were sick, and I stepped in to cheer you up a little. My friends often say: "It's such a comfort to see you, Aunty Doleful. You have such a flow of conversation, and are so lively." Besides, I said to myself, as I came up the stairs: "Perhaps it's the last time I'll ever see Cornelia Jane alive."

You don't mean to die yet, eh? Well, now, how do you know? You can't tell. You think you are getting better, but there was poor Mrs. Jones sitting up, and every one saying how smart she was, and all of a sudden she was taken with spasms in the heart, and went off like a flash. Parthenia is young to bring the baby up by hand. But you must be careful, and not get anxious or excited. Keep quite calm, and don't fret about anything. Of course, things can't go on jest as if you were down-stairs; and I wondered whether you knew your little Billy was sailing about in a tub on the mill-pond, and that your little Sammy was letting your little Jimmy down from the veranda-roof in a clothes-basket.

Gracious goodness, what's the matter? I guess Providence'll take care of 'em. Don't look so. You thought Bridget was watching them? Well, no, she isn't. I saw her talking to a man at the gate. He looked to me like a burglar. No doubt she'll let him take the impression of the door-key in wax, and then he'll get in and murder you all. There was a family at Bobble Hill all killed last week for fifty dollars. Now, don't fidget so; it will be bad for the baby.

Poor, little dear! How singular it is, to be sure, that you can't tell whether a child is blind, or deaf and dumb, or a cripple at that age. It might be all, and you'd never know it.

Most of them that have their senses make bad use of them though; that ought to be your comfort, if it does turn out to have anything dreadful the matter with it. And more don't live a year. I saw a baby's funeral down the street as I came along.

How is Mr. Kobble? Well, but finds it warm in town, eh? Well, I should think he would. They are dropping down by hundreds there with sun-stroke. You must prepare your mind to have him brought home any day. Anyhow, a trip on these railroad trains is just risking your life every time you take one. Back and forth every day as he is, it's just trifling with danger.

Dear! dear! now to think what dreadful things hang over us all the time! Dear! dear!

Scarlet fever has broken out in the village, Cornelia. Little Isaac Potter has it, and I saw your Jimmy playing with him last Saturday.

Well, I must be going now. I've got another sick friend, and I sha'n't think my duty done unless I cheer her up a little before I sleep. Good-by. How pale you look, Cornelia! I don't believe you have a good doctor. Do send him away and try some one else. You don't look so well as you did when I came in. But if anything happens, send for me at once. If I can't do anything else, I can cheer you up a little.

* * * * *

Mrs. Dallas, who lives in New York City, is a regular correspondent of the New York Ledger, having taken Fanny Fern's place on that widely circulated paper, is a prominent member of "Sorosis," and her Tuesday evening receptions draw about her some of the brightest society of that cosmopolitan centre.

All these selections are prizes for the long-suffering elocutionist who is expected to entertain his friends with something new, laughter-provoking, and fully up to the mark.

* * * * *

Mrs. Ames, of Brooklyn, known to the public as "Eleanor Kirk," has revealed in her "Thanksgiving Growl" a bit of honest experience, refreshing with its plain Saxon and homely realism, which, when recited with proper spirit, is most effective.

A THANKSGIVING GROWL.

Oh, dear! do put some more chips on the fire, And hurry up that oven! Just my luck-- To have the bread slack. Set that plate up higher! And for goodness' sake do clear this truck Away! Frogs' legs and marbles on my moulding-board! What next I wonder? John Henry, wash your face; And do get out from under foot, "Afford more Cream?" Used all you had? If that's the case, Skim all the pans. Do step a little spryer! I wish I hadn't asked so many folks To spend Thanksgiving. Good gracious! poke the fire And put some water on. Lord, how it smokes! I never was so tired in all my life! And there's the cake to frost, and dough to mix For tarts. I can't cut pumpkin with this knife! Some women's husbands know enough to fix The kitchen tools; but, for all mine would care, I might tear pumpkin with my teeth. John Henry, If you don't plant yourself on that 'ere chair, I'll set you down so hard that you'll agree You're stuck for good. Them cranberries are sour, And taste like gall beside. Hand me some flour, And do fly round. John Henry, wipe your nose! I wonder how 'twill be when I am dead? "How my nose'll be?" Yes, how your nose'll be, And how your back'll be. If that ain't red I'll miss my guess. I don't expect you'll see-- You nor your father neither--what I've done And suffered in this house. As true's I live Them pesky fowl ain't stuffed! The biggest one Will hold two loaves of bread. Say, wipe that sieve, And hand it here. You are the slowest poke In all Fairmount. Lor'! there's Deacon Gubben's wife! She'll be here to-morrow. That pan can soak A little while. I never in my life Saw such a lazy critter as she is. If she stayed home, there wouldn't be a thing To eat. You bet she'll fill up here! "It's riz?" Well, so it has. John Henry! Good king! How did that boy get out? You saw him go With both fists full of raisins and a pile Behind him, and you never let me know! There! you've talked so much I clean forgot the rye. I wonder if the Governor had to slave As I do, if he would be so pesky fresh about Thanksgiving Day? He'd been in his grave With half my work. What, get along without An Indian pudding? Well, that would be A novelty. No friend or foe shall say I'm close, or haven't as much variety As other folks. There! I think I see my way Quite clear. The onions are to peel. Let's see: Turnips, potatoes, apples there to stew, This squash to bake, and lick John Henry! And after that--I really think I'm through.

CHAPTER VII.

PROSE, BUT NOT PROSY.

Mrs. Alice Wellington Rollins, in those interesting articles in the Critic which induced me to look further, says:

"We claim high rank for the humor of women because it is almost exclusively of this higher, imaginative type. A woman rarely tells an anecdote, or hoards up a good story, or comes in and describes to you something funny that she has seen. Her humor is like a flash of lightning from a clear sky, coming when you least expect it, when it could not have been premeditated, and when, to the average consciousness, there is not the slightest provocation to humor, possessing thus in the very highest degree that element of surprise which is not only a factor in all humor, but to our mind the most important factor. You tell her that you cannot spend the winter with her because you have promised to spend it with some one else, and she exclaims: 'Oh, Ellen! why were you not born twins!' She has, perhaps, recently built for herself a most charming home, and coming to see yours, which happens to be just a trifle more luxurious and charming, she remarks as she turns away: 'All I can say is, when you want to see squalor, come and visit me in Oxford Street!' She puts down her heavy coffee-cup of stone-china with its untasted coffee at a little country inn, saying, with a sigh: 'It's no use; I can't get at it; it's like trying to drink over a stone wall.' She writes in a letter: 'We parted this morning with mutual satisfaction; that is, I suppose we did; I know my satisfaction was mutual enough for two.' She asks her little restless daughter in the most insinuating tones if she would not like to sit in papa's lap and have him tell her a story; and when the little daughter responds with a most uncompromising 'no!' turns her inducement into a threat, and remarks with severity: 'Well, be a good girl, or you will have to!' She complains, when you have kept her waiting while you were buying undersleeves, that you must have bought 'undersleeves enough for a centipede.' You ask how poor Mr. X---- is--the disconsolate widower who a fortnight ago was completely prostrated by his wife's death, and are told in calm and even tones that he is 'beginning to take notice.' You tell her that one of the best fellows in the class has been unjustly expelled, and that the class are to wear crape on their left arms for thirty days, and that you only hope that the President will meet you in the college-yard and ask why you wear it; to all of which she replies soothingly, 'I wouldn't do that, Henry; for the President might tell you not to mourn, as your friend was not lost, only gone before.' You tell her of your stunned sensation on finding some of your literary work complimented in the Nation, and she exclaims: 'I should think so! It must be like meeting an Indian and seeing him put his hand into his no-pocket to draw out a scented pocket-handkerchief, instead of a tomahawk.' Or she writes that two Sunday-schools are trying to do all the good they can, but that each is determined at any cost to do more good than the other."

* * * * *

I have selected several specimens of this higher type of humor.

Mrs. Ellen H. Rollins was pre-eminently gifted in this direction. The humor in her exquisite "New England Bygones" is so interwoven with the simple pathos of her memories that it cannot be detached without detriment to both. But I will venture to select three sketches from

OLD-TIME CHILD LIFE.

BY E.H. ARR.

Betsy had the reddest hair of any girl I ever knew. It was quite short in front, and she had a way of twisting it, on either temple, into two little buttons, which she fastened with pins. The rest of it she brought quite far up on the top of her head, where she kept it in place with a large-sized horn comb. Her face was covered with freckles, and her eyes, in winter, were apt to be inflamed. She always seemed to have a mop in her hand, and she had no respect for paint. She was as neat as old Dame Safford herself, and was continually "straightening things out," as she called it. Her temper, like her hair, was somewhat fiery; and when her work did not suit her, she was prone to a gloomy view of life. If she was to be believed, things were always "going to wrack and ruin" about the house; and she had a queer way of taking time by the forelock. In the morning it was "going on to twelve o'clock," and at noon it was "going on to midnight."

She kept her six kitchen chairs in a row on one side of the room, and as many flatirons in a line on the mantelpiece. Everything where she was had, she said, to "stand just so;" and woe to the child who carried crookedness into her straight lines! Betsy had a manner of her own, and made a wonderful kind of a courtesy, with which her skirts puffed out all around like a cheese. She always courtesied to Parson Meeker when she met him, and said: "I hope to see you well, sir." Once she courtesied in a prayer-meeting to a man who offered her a chair, and told him, in a shrill voice, to "keep his setting," though she was "ever so much obleeged" to him. This was when she was under conviction, and Parson Meeker said he thought she had met with a change of heart. Father Lathem's wife hoped so too, for then "there would be a chance of having some Long-noses and Pudding-sweets left over in the orchard."

It was in time of the long drought, when fire ran over Grayface, and a great comet appeared in the sky. Some of the people of Whitefield thought the world was coming to an end. The comet stayed for weeks, visible even at noon-day, stretching its tail from the zenith far toward the western horizon, and at night staring in at windows with its eye of fire. It was the talk of the people, who pondered over it with a helpless wonder. I recall two Whitefield women as they stood, one morning, bare-armed in a doorway, staring at and chattering about it. One says they "might as well stop work" and "take it easy" while they can. The other thinks the better way is to "keep on a stiddy jog until it comes." They wish they knew "how near it is," and "what the tail means anyway."

Betsy comes along with a pail, which she sets down, and then looks up to the comet. The air is dense with smoke from Grayface, and the dry earth is full of cracks. Betsy declares that it is "going on two months since there has been any rain." Everything is "going to wrack and ruin," and "if that thing up there should burst, there'll be an end to Whitefield."

Then she catches sight of me listening wide-mouthed, and she tells me that I needn't suppose she is "going home to iron my pink muslin," for she thinks the tail of the comet "has started, and is coming right down to whisk it off from the line." I believe her, and distinctly remember the terror that took hold of me as I rushed home and tore the pink muslin from the line, lest it should be whisked off by the comet's tail.

When the drought broke, a single day's rain washed all the smoke from the air. Directly, the tail of the comet began to fade, and all of a sudden its fiery eye went out of the sky.

Some of the villagers thought it had "burst," others that it had "burned out." Betsy said: "Whatever it was, it was a humbug;" and the wisest man in Whitefield could neither tell whence it came nor whither it went. One thing, however, was certain: Farmer Lathem said that never, since his orchard began to bear, had he gathered such a crop of apples as he did, despite the drought, in the year of the great comet.

MRS. MEEKER.

BY E.H. ARR.

When I read of Roman matrons I always think of Mrs. Meeker. Her features were marked, and her eyes of deepest blue. She wore her hair combed closely down over her ears, so that her forehead seemed to run up in a point high upon her head: Its color was of reddish-brown, and, I am sorry to say, so far as it was seen, it was not her own. It was called a scratch, and Betsy said Mrs. Meeker "would look enough sight better if she would leave it off." Whether any hair at all grew upon Mrs. Meeker's head was a great problem with the village children, and nothing could better illustrate the dignity of this woman than the fact that for more than thirty years the whole neighborhood tried in vain to find out.

PARSON MEEKER.

BY E.H. ARR.

Every Sunday he preached two long sermons, each with five heads, and each head itself divided. After the fifthly came an application, with an exhortation at its close. The sermons were called very able, or, more often, "strong discourses." I used to think this was because Mrs. Meeker had stitched their leaves fast together. Betsy said they were just like Deacon Saunders's breaking-up plough, "and went tearing right through sin." The parson, when I knew him, was a little slow of speech and dull of sight. He sometimes lost his place on his page. How afraid I used to be lest, not finding it, he should repeat his heads! He always brought himself up with a jerk, however, and sailed safely through to the application.

When that came, Benny almost always gave me a jog with his elbow or foot. Once he stuck a pin into my arm, which made me jump so that Deacon Saunders, who sat behind, waked up with a loud snort. The deacon was always talking about the sermons being "powerful in doctrine." When Benny asked Betsy what doctrines were, she told him to "let doctrines alone;" that they were "pizen things, only fit for hardened old sinners."

* * * * *

There are many delightful articles which must be merely alluded to in passing, as the "Old Salem Shops," by Eleanor Putnam, so delicate and delicious that, once read, it will ever be a fragrant memory; Louise Stockton's "Woman in the Restaurant" I want to give you, and Mrs. Barrow's "Pennikitty People;" a chapter from Miss Baylor's "On This Side," and the opening chapters of Miss Phelps's "Old Maids' Paradise;" also the description of "Joppa," by Grace Denio Litchfield, in "Only an Incident." There are others from which it is not possible to make extracts. Miss Woolson's admirable "For the Major," though pathetic, almost tragic, in its underlying feeling, is, at the same time, a story of exquisite humor, from which, nevertheless, not a single sentence could be quoted that would be called "funny." Her work, and that of Frances Hodgson Burnett, as well as that of Miss Phelps and Mrs. Spofford, shine with a silver thread of humor, worked too intimately into the whole warp and woof to be extracted without injuring both the solid material and the tinsel. To appreciate the point and delicacy of their finest wit, you must read the whole story and grasp the entire character or situation.

Mrs. E.W. Bellamy, a Southern lady, published in last year's Atlantic Monthly a sketch called "At Bent's Hotel," which ought to have a place in this volume; but my publisher says authoritatively that there must be a limit somewhere; so this gem must be included in--a second series!

* * * * *

There is so much truth as well as humor in the following article, that it must be included. It gives in prose the agonies which Saxe told so feelingly in verse:

A FATAL REPUTATION.

BY ISABEL FRANCES BELLOWS.

I am impelled to write this as an awful warning to young men and women who are just entering upon life and its responsibilities. Years ago I thoughtlessly took a false step, which at the time seemed trivial and of little import, but which has since assumed colossal proportions that threaten to overshadow much of the innocent happiness of my otherwise placid existence. What wonder, then, that I try to avert this danger from young and inexperienced minds who in their gay thoughtlessness rush into the very jaws of the disaster, and before they are well aware find they are entrapped for life, as there is no escape for those who have thus brought their doom upon themselves.

I will try and relate how, like the Lady of Shalott, when I first began to gaze upon the world of realities "the curse" came upon me. It was in this wise:

I lived in my youth an almost cloistral life of seclusion and self-absorption, from which I was suddenly shaken by circumstances, and forced to mingle in the busy world; to which, after the first shock, I was not at all averse, but found very interesting, and also--and there was the weight that pulled me down--tolerably amusing. For I met some curious people, and saw and heard some remarkable things; and as I went among my friends I often used to give an account of my observations, until at last I discovered that wherever I went, and under whatever circumstances (except, of course, at the funeral of a member of the family), I was expected to be amusing! I found myself in the same relation to society that the clown bears to the circus-master who has engaged him--he must either be funny or leave the troupe.

Now, I am unfortunate in having no particular accomplishments. I cannot sing either the old songs or the new; neither am I a performer on divers instruments. I can paint a little, but my paintings do not seem to rouse any enthusiasm in the beholder, nor do they add an inspiring strain to conversation. I can, indeed, make gingerbread and six different kinds of pudding, but I hesitate to mention it, because the cook is far in advance of me in all these particulars, not to mention numerous other ways in which she excels. I have thus but one resource in life; and when I give one or two instances of the humiliation and distress of mind to which I have been subjected on its account I am sure I shall win a sympathizing thought even from those who are more favored by nature, and possibly save a few young spirits from the pain of treading in my footsteps.

In the first place, I am not naturally witty. Epigrams do not rise spontaneously to my lips, and it sometimes takes days and even weeks of consideration after an opportunity of making one has occurred before the appropriate words finally dawn upon me. By that time, of course, the retort is what the Catholics call "a work of supererogation." I perhaps possess a slight "sense of the humorous," which has undoubtedly given rise to the fatal demand upon me, but I do not remember ever having been very funny. There never was any danger of my experiencing difficulties like Dr. Holmes on that famous occasion when he was as funny as he could be. I have often been as funny as I could be, but the smallest of buttons on the slenderest of threads never detached itself on my account. I have never had to restrain my humorous remarks in the slightest degree, but on the contrary have sometimes been driven into making the most atrocious jokes, and even puns, because it was evident something of the sort was expected from me--only, of course, something better.

One occurrence of this kind will remain forever fixed in my memory. I was invited to a picnic, that most ghastly device of the human mind for playing at having a good time. At first I had declined to go, but it was represented to me that no less than three families had company for whose entertainment something must be done; that two young and interesting friends of mine just about to be engaged to each other would be simply inconsolable if the plan were given up; and, in short, that I should show by not going an extremely hateful and unseemly spirit--"besides, it wouldn't do to have it without you, my dear," continued my amiable friend, "because you know you are always the life of the party." So I sighed and consented.

The day arrived, and before nine o'clock in the morning the mercury stood at ninety degrees in the shade. The cook overslept herself, and breakfast was so late that William Henry missed the train into the city, which didn't make it pleasanter for any of us. I had made an especially delicate cake to take with me as my share of the feast, and while we were at breakfast I heard a crash in the direction of the kitchen, and hastening tremblingly to discover the origin of it I found the cake and the plate containing it in one indistinguishable heap on the floor.

"It slipped between me two hands as if it was alive, bad luck to it," said the cook; "and it was meself that saw the heavy crack in the plate before you set the cake onto it, mum!"

I took cookies and boiled eggs to the picnic.

The wreck had hardly been cleared away before my son and heir appeared in the doorway with a hole of unimagined dimensions in his third worst trousers. His second worst were already in the mending basket, so nothing remained for me but to clothe him in his best suit and wonder all day in which part of them I should find the largest hole when I came home.

Lastly, I had just put on my hat, and was preparing to set forth, warm, tired and demoralized, when my youngest, in her anxiety to bid me a sufficiently affectionate farewell, lost her small balance, and came rolling down-stairs after me. No serious harm was done, but it took nearly an hour before I succeeded in soothing and comforting her sufficiently to be able to leave her, with two brown-paper patches on her head and elbow, in the care of the nurse.

When I arrived late, discouraged and with a headache, at the picnic grounds, I found the assembled company sitting vapidly about among mosquitoes and beetles, already looking bored to death, and I soon perceived that it was expected of me to provide amusement and entertainment for the crowd. I tried to rally, therefore, and proposed a few games, which went off in a spiritless manner enough, and apparently in consequence I began to be assailed with questions and remarks of a reproachful character.

"Don't you feel well to-day?" "Has anything happened?" "You don't seem as lively as usual!" No one took the slightest notice of my explanations, until at last, goaded into desperation by one evil-minded old woman, who asked me if it were true that my husband was involved in the failure of Smith, Jones & Co., I launched out and became wildly and disgracefully silly. Nothing seemed too foolish, too senseless to say if it only answered the great purpose of keeping off the attack of personal questions.

Thus the wretched day wore on, until at last it was time to go home, and the first feeling approaching content was stealing into my weary bosom as I gathered up my basket and shawls, when it was rudely dashed by the following conversation, conducted by two ladies to whom I had been introduced that day. They were standing at a little distance from the rest of the company and from me, and evidently thought themselves far enough away to talk quite loud, so that these words were plainly borne to my ears:

"I hate to see people try to make themselves so conspicuous, don't you?"

"Yes, indeed; and to try to be funny when they haven't any fun in them."

"I can't imagine what Maria was thinking about to call her witty!"

"I know it. I should think such people had better keep quiet when they haven't anything to say. I'm glad it's time to go home. Picnics are such stupid things!"

What more was said I do not know, for I left the spot as quickly as possible, making an inward resolution to avoid all picnics in the future till I should arrive at my second childhood.

I cannot refrain from giving one other little instance of my sufferings from this cause. I was again invited out; this time to a lunch party, specially to meet the friend of a friend of mine. The very morning of the day it was to take place I received a telegram stating that my great-aunt had died suddenly in California. Now people don't usually care much about their great-aunts. They can bear to be chastened in this direction very comfortably; but I did care about mine. She had been very kind to me, and though the width of a continent had separated us for the last ten years her memory was still dear to me.

I sat down immediately to write a note excusing myself from my friend's lunch party, when, just as I took the paper, it occurred to me that it was rather a selfish thing to do. My friend's guests were invited, and her arrangements all made; and as the visit of her friend was to be very short the opportunity of our meeting would probably be lost. So I wrote instead a note to the daughter of my great aunt, and when the time came I went to the lunch party with a heavy heart. I had no opportunity of telling my friend of the sad news I had received that morning, and I suppose I may have been quiet; perhaps I even seemed indifferent, though I tried not to be. I could not have been very successful, however, for I was just going up-stairs to put on my "things" to go home, when I heard this little conversation in the dressing-room:

"It's too bad she wasn't more interesting to-day, but you never can tell how it will be. She will do as she likes, and that's the end of it."

"Yes," said another voice, "I think she is rather a moody person anyway; she won't say a word if she doesn't feel like it."

"'Sh--'sh--here she comes," said another, with the tone and look that told me it was I of whom they were talking.

And so I adjure all youthful and hopeful persons, who have a tendency to be funny, to keep it a profound secret from the world. Indulge in your propensities to any extent in your family circle; keep your immediate relatives, if you like, in convulsions of inextinguishable laughter all the time; but when you mingle in society guard your secret with your life. Never make a joke, and, if necessary, never take one; and by so doing you shall peradventure escape that wrath to come to which I have fallen an innocent victim, and which I doubt not will bring me to an untimely end.--The Independent.

* * * * *

And a few pages from Miss Murfree, who has shown such rare power in her short character sketches.

A BLACKSMITH IN LOVE.

BY CHARLES EGBERT CRADDOCK.

The pine-knots flamed and glistened under the great wash-kettle. A tree-toad was persistently calling for rain in the dry distance. The girl, gravely impassive, beat the clothes with the heavy paddle. Her mother shortly ceased to prod the white heaps in the boiling water, and presently took up the thread of her discourse.

"An' 'Vander hev got ter be a mighty suddint man. I hearn tell, when I war down ter M'ria's house ter the quiltin', ez how in that sorter fight an' scrimmage they hed at the mill las' month, he war powerful ill-conducted. Nobody hed thought of hevin' much of a fight--thar hed been jes' a few licks passed atwixt the men thar; but the fust finger ez war laid on this boy, he jes' lit out, an' fit like a catamount. Right an' lef' he lay about him with his fists, an' he drawed his huntin'-knife on some of 'em. The men at the mill war in no wise pleased with him."

"'Pears like ter me ez 'Vander air a peaceable boy enough, ef he ain't jawed at an' air lef' be," drawled Cynthia.

Her mother was embarrassed for a moment. Then, with a look both sly and wise, she made an admission--a qualified admission. "Waal, wimmen--ef--ef--ef they air young an' toler'ble hard-headed yit, air likely ter jaw some, ennyhow. An' a gal oughtn't ter marry a man ez hev sot his heart on bein' lef' in peace. He is apt ter be a mighty sour an' disapp'inted critter."

This sudden turn to the conversation invested all that had been said with new meaning, and revealed a subtle diplomatic intention. The girl seemed deliberately to review it as she paused in her work. Then, with a rising flush: "I ain't studyin' 'bout marryin' nobody," she asserted staidly. "I hev laid off ter live single."

Mrs. Ware had overshot the mark, but she retorted, gallantly reckless: "That's what yer Aunt Malviny useter declar' fur gospel sure, when she war a gal. An' she hev got ten chil'ren, an' hev buried two husbands; an' ef all they say air true, she's tollin' in the third man now. She's a mighty spry, good-featured woman, an' a fust-rate manager, yer Aunt Malviny air, an' both her husbands lef' her suthin--cows, or wagons, or land. An' they war quiet men when they war alive, an' stays whar they air put now that they air dead; not like old Parson Hoodenpyle, what his wife hears stumpin' round the house an' preachin' every night, though she air ez deef ez a post, an' he hev been in glory twenty year--twenty year an' better. Yer Aunt Malviny hed luck, so mebbe 'tain't no killin' complaint fur a gal ter git ter talking like a fool about marryin' an' sech. Leastwise I ain't minded ter sorrow."

She looked at her daughter with a gay grin, which, distorted by her toothless gums and the wreathing steam from the kettle, enhanced her witch-like aspect and was spuriously malevolent. She did not notice the stir of an approach through the brambly tangles of the heights above until it was close at hand; as she turned, she thought only of the mountain cattle and to see the red cow's picturesque head and crumpled horns thrust over the sassafras bushes, or to hear the brindle's clanking bell. It was certainly less unexpected to Cynthia when a young mountaineer, clad in brown jean trousers and a checked homespun shirt, emerged upon the rocky slope. He still wore his blacksmith's leather apron, and his powerful corded hammer-arm was bare beneath his tightly-rolled sleeve. He was tall and heavily built; his sunburned face was square, with a strong lower jaw, and his features were accented by fine lines of charcoal, as if the whole were a clever sketch.

His black eyes held fierce intimations, but there was mobility of expression about them that suggested changing impulses, strong but fleeting. He was like his forge-fire; though the heat might be intense for a time, it fluctuated with the breath of the bellows. Just now he was meekly quailing before the old woman, whom he evidently had not thought to find here. It was as apt an illustration as might be, perhaps, of the inferiority of strength to finesse. She seemed an inconsiderable adversary, as, haggard, lean, and prematurely aged, she swayed on her prodding-stick about the huge kettle; but she was as a veritable David to this big young Goliath, though she, too, flung hardly more than a pebble at him.

"Laws-a-me!" she cried, in shrill, toothless glee; "ef hyar ain't 'Vander Price! What brung ye down hyar along o' we-uns, 'Vander?" she continued, with simulated anxiety. "Hev that thar red heifer o' ourn lept over the fence agin, an' got inter Pete's corn? Waal, sir, ef she ain't the headin'est heifer!"

"I hain't seen none o' yer heifer, ez I knows on," replied the young blacksmith, with gruff, drawling deprecation. Then he tried to regain his natural manner. "I kem down hyar," he remarked, in an off-hand way, "ter git a drink o' water." He glanced furtively at the girl, then looked quickly away at the gallant red-bird, still gayly parading among the leaves.

The old woman grinned with delight. "Now, ef that ain't s'prisin'," she declared. "Ef we hed knowed ez Lost Creek war a-goin' dry over yander a-nigh the shop, so ye an' Pete would hev ter kem hyar thirstin' fur water, we-uns would hev brung suthin' down hyar ter drink out'n. We-uns hain't got no gourd hyar, hev we, Cynthy?"

"'Thout it air the little gourd with the saft-soap in it," said Cynthia, confused and blushing. Her mother broke into a high, loud laugh.

"Ye ain't wantin' ter gin 'Vander the soap-gourd ter drink out'n, Cynthy! Leastwise, I ain't goin' ter gin it ter Pete. Fur I s'pose ef ye hev ter kem a haffen mile ter git a drink, 'Vander, ez surely Pete'll hev ter kem, too. Waal, waal, who would hev b'lieved ez Lost Creek would go dry nigh the shop, an' yit be a-scuttlin' along like that hyarabouts!" and she pointed with her bony finger at the swift flow of the water.

He was forced to abandon his clumsy pretence of thirst. "Lost Creek ain't gone dry nowhar, ez I knows on," he admitted, mechanically rolling the sleeve of his hammer-arm up and down as he talked.

* * * * *

From Miss Woolson's story of "Anne," I give the pen-portrait of the precise

"MISS LOIS."

"Codfish balls for breakfast on Sunday morning, of course," said Miss Lois, "and fried hasty-pudding. On Wednesdays, a boiled dinner. Pies on Tuesdays and Saturdays."

The pins stood in straight rows on her pincushion; three times each week every room in the house was swept, and the floors, as well as the furniture, dusted. Beans were baked in an iron pot on Saturday night, and sweet-cake was made on Thursday. Winter or summer, through scarcity or plenty, Miss

Lois never varied her established routine, thereby setting an example, she said, to the idle and shiftless. And certainly she was a faithful guide-post, continually pointing out an industrious and systematic way, which, however, to the end of time, no French-blooded, French-hearted person will ever travel, unless dragged by force. The villagers preferred their lake trout to Miss Lois's salt codfish, their tartines to her corn-meal puddings, and their eau-de-vie to her green tea; they loved their disorder and their comfort; her bar soap and scrubbing-brush were a horror to their eyes. They washed the household clothes two or three times a year. Was not that enough? Of what use the endless labor of this sharp-nosed woman, with glasses over her eyes, at the church-house? Were not, perhaps, the glasses the consequence of such toil? And her figure of a long leanness also?

The element of real heroism, however, came into Miss Lois's life in her persistent effort to employ Indian servants. Through long years had she persisted, through long years would she continue to persist. A succession of Chippewa squaws broke, stole, and skirmished their way through her kitchen, with various degrees of success, generally in the end departing suddenly at night with whatever booty they could lay their hands on. It is but justice to add, however, that this was not much, a rigid system of keys and excellent locks prevailing in the well-watched household. Miss Lois's conscience would not allow her to employ half-breeds, who were sometimes endurable servants; duty required, she said, that she should have full-blooded natives. And she had them. She always began to teach them the alphabet within three days after their arrival, and the spectacle of a tearful, freshly-caught Indian girl, very wretched in her calico dress and white apron, worn out with the ways of the kettles and the brasses, dejected over the fish-balls, and appalled by the pudding, standing confronted by a large alphabet on the well-scoured table, and Miss Lois by her side with a pointer, was frequent and even regular in its occurrence, the only change being in the personality of the learners. No one of them had ever gone through the letters, but Miss Lois was not discouraged.

THE CIRCUS AT DENBY.

BY SARAH ORNE JEWETT.

I cannot truthfully say that it was a good show; it was somewhat dreary, now that I think of it quietly and without excitement. The creatures looked tired, and as if they had been on the road for a great many years. The animals were all old, and there was a shabby great elephant whose look of general discouragement went to my heart, for it seemed as if he were miserably conscious of a misspent life. He stood dejected and motionless at one side of the tent, and it was hard to believe that there was a spark of vitality left in him. A great number of the people had never seen an elephant before, and we heard a thin, little old man, who stood near us, say delightedly: "There's the old creatur', and no mistake, Ann 'Liza. I wanted to see him most of anything. My sakes alive, ain't he big!"

And Ann 'Liza, who was stout and sleepy-looking, droned out: "Ye-es, there's consider'ble of him; but he looks as if he ain't got no animation."

Kate and I turned away and laughed, while Mrs. Kew said, confidentially, as the couple moved away: "She needn't be a reflectin' on the poor beast. That's Mis' Seth Tanner, and there isn't a woman in Deep Haven nor East Parish to be named the same day with her for laziness. I'm glad she didn't catch sight of me; she'd have talked about nothing for a fortnight." There was a picture of a huge snake in Deep Haven, and I was just wondering where he could be, or if there ever had been one, when we heard a boy ask the same question of the man whose thankless task it was to stir up the lions with a stick to make them roar. "The snake's dead," he answered, good-naturedly. "Didn't you have to dig an awful long grave for him?" asked the boy; but the man said he reckoned they curled him up some, and smiled as he turned to his lions, that looked as if they needed a tonic. Everybody lingered longest before the monkeys, that seemed to be the only lively creatures in the whole collection....

Coming out of the great tent was disagreeable enough, and we seemed to have chosen the worst time, for the crowd pushed fiercely, though I suppose nobody was in the least hurry, and we were all severely jammed, while from somewhere underneath came the wails of a deserted dog. We had not meant to see the side shows; but when we came in sight of the picture of the Kentucky giantess, we noticed that Mrs. Kew looked at it wistfully, and we immediately asked if she cared anything about going to see the wonder, whereupon she confessed that she never heard of such a thing as a woman's weighing six hundred and fifty pounds; so we all three went in. There were only two or three persons inside the tent, beside a little boy who played the hand-organ.

The Kentucky giantess sat in two chairs on a platform, and there was a large cage of monkeys just beyond, toward which Kate and I went at once. "Why, she isn't more than two thirds as big as the picture," said Mrs. Kew, in a regretful whisper; "but I guess she's big enough; doesn't she look discouraged, poor creatur'?" Kate and I felt ashamed of ourselves for being there. No matter if she had consented to be carried round for a show, it must have been horrible to be stared at and joked about day after day; and we gravely looked at the monkeys, and in a few minutes turned to see if Mrs. Kew were not ready to come away, when, to our surprise, we saw that she was talking to the giantess with great interest, and we went nearer.

"I thought your face looked natural the minute I set foot inside the door," said Mrs. Kew; "but you've altered some since I saw you, and I couldn't place you till I heard you speak. Why, you used to be spare. I am amazed, Marilly! Where are your folks?"

"I don't wonder you are surprised," said the giantess. "I was a good ways from this when you knew me, wasn't I? But father, he ran through with every cent he had before he died, and 'he' took to drink, and it killed him after a while; and then I begun to grow worse and worse, till I couldn't do nothing to earn a dollar, and everybody was a-coming to see me, till at last I used to ask 'em ten cents apiece, and I scratched along somehow till this man came round and heard of me; and he offered me my keep and good pay to go along with him. He had another giantess before me, but she had begun to fall away considerable, so he paid her off and let her go. This other giantess was an awful expense to him, she was such an eater; now, I don't have no great of an appetite"--this was said plaintively--"and he's raised my pay since I've been with him because we did so well."...

"Have you been living in Kentucky long?" asked Mrs. Kew. "I saw it on the picture outside."

"No," said the giantess; "that was a picture the man bought cheap from another show that broke up last year. It says six hundred and fifty pounds, but I don't weigh more than four hundred. I haven't been weighed for some time past. Between you and me, I don't weigh as much as that, but you mustn't mention it, for it would spoil my reputation and might hinder my getting another engagement."

Then they shook hands in a way that meant a great deal, and when Kate and I said good-afternoon, the giantess looked at us gratefully, and said: "I'm very much obliged to you for coming in, young ladies."

"Walk in! Walk in!" the man was shouting as we came away. "Walk in and see the wonder of the world, ladies and gentlemen--the largest woman ever seen in America--the great Kentucky giantess!"

NEW YORK TO NEWPORT.

A Trip of Trials.

BY LOUISE CHANDLER MOULTON.

The Jane Moseley was a disappointment--most Janes are. If they had called her Samuel, no doubt she would have behaved better; but they called her Jane, and the natural consequences of our mistakes cannot be averted from ourselves or others. A band was playing wild strains of welcome as we approached. Come and sail with us, it said--it is summer, and the days are long. Care is of the land--here the waves flow, and the winds blow, and captain smiles, and stewardess beguiles, and all is music, music, music. How the wild, exultant strains rose and fell--but everything rose and fell on that boat, as we found out afterward. Just here a spirit of justice falls on me, like the gentle dew from heaven, and forces me to admit that it rained like a young deluge; that it had been raining for two days, and the bosom of the deep was heaving with responsive sympathy; as what bosom would not on which so many tears had been shed? Perhaps responsive sympathy was the secret of the Jane Moseley's behavior; but I would her heart had been less tender. Then, too, the passengers were few; and of course as we had to divide the roll and tumble between us, there was a great deal for each one.

There was a Pretty Girl, and she had a sister who was not pretty. It seemed to me that even the sad sea waves were kinder to the Pretty Girl, such is the influence of youth and beauty. There were various men--heavy swells I should call some of them, only that that would be slang; but heavy swells were the order of the day. Then there was a benevolent old lady who believed in everything--in the music, and the Jane Moseley, and the long days, and the summer. There was another old lady of restless mind, who evidently believed in nothing, hoped for nothing, expected nothing. She tried all the lounges and all the corners, and found each one a separate disappointment. There was a fat, fair one, of friendly face, and beside her her grim guardian, a man so thin that you at once cast him for the part of Starveling in this Midsummer Day's Dream of Delusion.

We put out from shore--quite out of sight of shore, in short--and then the perfidious music ceased. To the people on land it had sung, "Come and make merry with us," but from us, trying in vain to make merry, it withheld its deceitful inspiration. For the exceeding weight of sorrow that presently settled down upon us it had no balm. When you are on a pleasure trip it is unpleasant to be miserable; so I tried hard to shake off the mild melancholy that began to steal over me. I said to myself, I will not affront the great deep with my personal woes. I am but a woman, yet perhaps on this so great occasion magnanimity of soul will be possible even to me. I will consider my neighbors and be wise. At one end of the long saloon a banquet-board was spread. Its hospitality was, like the other attractions of the Jane Moseley, a perfidious pageant. Nobody sought its soup or claimed its clams. One or two sad-eyed young men made their way in that direction from time to time-- after their sea-legs, perhaps. From their gait when they came back I inferred they did not find them. The human nature in the saloon became a weariness to me. Even the gentle gambols of the dog Thaddeus, a sportive and spotted pointer in whom I had been interested, failed to soothe my perturbed spirits. De Quincey speaks somewhere of "the awful solitariness of every human soul." No wonder, then, that I should be solitary among the festive few on board the Jane Moseley--no wonder I felt myself darkly, deeply, desperately blue. I thought I would go on deck. I clung to my companion with an ardor which would have been flattering had it been voluntary. My faltering steps were guided to a seat just within the guards. I sat there thinking that I had never nursed a dear gazelle, so I could not be quite sure whether it would have died or not, but I thought it would. I mused on the changing fortunes of this unsteady world, and the ingratitude of man. I thought it would be easier going to the Promised Land if Jordan did not roll between. Rolling had long ceased to be a pleasant figure of speech with me. How frail are all things here below, how false, and yet how fair! My mind is naturally picturesque. In the midst of my sadness the force of nature compelled me to grope after an illustration. I could only think that my own foothold was frail, that the Jane Moseley was false, that the Pretty Girl was fair. A dizziness of brain resulted from this rhetorical effort. I silently confided my sorrows to the sympathizing bosom of the sea. I was soothed by the kindred melancholy of the sad sea waves. If the size of the waves were remarkable, other sighs abounded also, and other things waved--many of them.

True to my purpose of studying my fellow-beings, and learning wisdom by observation, I surveyed the Pretty Girl and her sister, who had by that time come on deck. They were surrounded by a group of audacious male creatures, who surrounded most on the side where the Pretty Girl sat. She did not look feeble. She was like the red, red rose. It was a conundrum to me why so much greater anxiety should be bestowed upon her health than upon her sister's. It needed some moral reflection to make it out; but I concluded that pretty girls were, by some law of nature, more subject to sea-sickness than plain ones; therefore, all these careful cares were quite in order. I saw the two old ladies--the benevolent one who had believed so implicitly in all things, but over whose benign visage doubt had now begun to settle like a cloud; and the other, who had hoped nothing from the first, and therefore over whom no disappointment could prevail--and, seeing, I mildly wondered whether, indeed, 'twere better to have loved and lost, or never to have loved at all.

My thoughts grew solemn. The green shores beyond the swelling flood seemed farther off than ever. The Jane Moseley had promised to land us at Newport pier at seven o'clock. It was already half-past seven; oh, perfidious Jane! Darkness had settled upon the face of the deep. We went inside. The sad-eyed young men had evidently been hunting for their sea-legs again, in the neighborhood of the banqueting-table, where nobody banqueted. Failing to find the secret of correct locomotion, they had laid themselves down to sleep, but in that sleep at sea what dreams did come, and how noisy they were! The dog Thaddeus walked by dejectedly, sniffing at the ghost of some half-forgotten joy. At last there rose a cry--Newport! The sleepers started to their feet. I started to mine, but I discreetly and quietly sat down again. Was it Newport, at last? Not at all. The harbor lights were gleaming from afar; and the cry was of the bandmaster shouting to his emissaries, arousing fiddle and flute and bassoon to their deceitful duty. They had played us out of port--

they would play us in again. They had promised us that all should go merry as a marriage-bell, and--I would not be understood to complain, but it had been a sad occasion. Now the deceitful strains rose and fell again upon the salt sea wind. The many lights glowed and twinkled from the near shore. We are all at play, come and play with us, screamed the soft waltz music. It is summer, and the days are long, and trouble is not, and care is banished. If the waves sigh, it is with bliss. Our voyage is ended. It is sad that you did not sail with us, but we will invite you again to-morrow, and the band shall play, and the crowd be gay, and airs beguile, and blue skies smile, and all shall be music, music, music. But I have sailed with you, on a summer day, bland master of a faithless band; and I know how soon your pipes are dumb--I know the tricks and manners of the clouds and the wind, and the swelling sea, and Jane Moseley, the perfidious.

I must, after all, have strong local attachments, for when at last the time came to land I left the ship with lingering reluctance. My feet seemed fastened to the deck where I had made my brief home on the much rolling deep. I had grown used to pain and resigned to fate. I walked the plank unsteadily. I stood on shore amid the rain and the mist. A hackman preyed upon me. I was put into an ancient ark and trundled on through the queer, irresolute, contradictory old streets, beside the lovely bay, all aglow with the lighted yachts, as a Southern swamp is with fire-flies. A torchlight procession met and escorted me. To this hour I am at a loss to know whether this attention was a delicate tribute on the part of the city of Newport to a distinguished guest, or a parting attention from the company who sail the Jane Moseley, and advertise in the Tribune--a final subterfuge to persuade a tortured passenger, by means of this transitory glory, that the sail upon a summer sea had been a pleasure trip.--Letter to New York Tribune.

CHAPTER VIII.

HUMOROUS POEMS.

I will next group a score of poems and doggerel rhymes with their various degrees of humor.

THE FIRST NEEDLE.

BY LUCRETIA P. HALE.

"Have you heard the new invention, my dears, That a man has invented?" said she. "It's a stick with an eye Through which you can tie A thread so long, it acts like a thong, And the men have such fun, To see the thing run! A firm, strong thread, through that eye at the head, Is pulled over the edges most craftily, And makes a beautiful seam to see!"

"What, instead of those wearisome thorns, my dear, Those wearisome thorns?" cried they. "The seam we pin Driving them in, But where are they by the end of the day, With dancing, and jumping, and leaps by the sea? For wintry weather They won't hold together, Seal-skins and bear-skins all dropping round Off from our shoulders down to the ground. The thorns, the tiresome thorns, will prick, But none of them ever consented to stick! Oh, won't the men let us this new thing use? If we mend their clothes they can't refuse. Ah, to sew up a seam for them to see-- What a treat, a delightful treat, 'twill be!"

"Yes, a nice thing, too, for the babies, my dears-- But, alas, there is but one!" cried she. "I saw them passing it round, and then They said it was fit for only men! What woman would know How to make the thing go? There was not a man so foolish to dream That any woman could sew up a seam!" Oh, then there was babbling and scrabbling, my dears! "At least they might let us do that!" cried they. "Let them shout and fight And kill bears all night; We'll leave them their spears and hatchets of stone If they'll give us this thing for our very own. It will be like a joy above all we could scheme, To sit up all night and sew such a seam."

"Beware! take care!" cried an aged old crone, "Take care what you promise," said she. "At first 'twill be fun, But, in the long run, You'll wish you had let the thing be. Through this stick with an eye I look and espy That for ages and ages you'll sit and you'll sew, And longer and longer the seams will grow, And you'll wish you never had asked to sew. But naught that I say Can keep back the day, For the men will return to their hunting and rowing, And leave to the women forever the sewing."

Ah, what are the words of an aged crone? For all have left her muttering alone; And the needle and thread that they got with such pains, They forever must keep as dagger and chains.

THE FUNNY STORY.

BY JOSEPHINE POLLARD.

It was such a funny story! how I wish you could have heard it, For it set us all a-laughing, from the little to the big; I'd really like to tell it, but I don't know how to word it, Though it travels to the music of a very lively jig.

If Sally just began it, then Amelia Jane would giggle, And Mehetable and Susan try their very broadest grin; And the infant Zachariah on his mother's lap would wriggle, And add a lusty chorus to the very merry din.

It was such a funny story, with its cheery snap and crackle, And Sally always told it with so much dramatic art, That the chickens in the door-yard would begin to "cackle-cackle," As if in such a frolic they were anxious to take part.

It was all about a--ha! ha!--and a--ho! ho! ho!--well really, It is--he! he! he!--I never could begin to tell you half Of the nonsense there was in it, for I just remember clearly It began with--ha! ha! ha! ha! and it ended with a laugh.

But Sally--she could tell it, looking at us so demurely, With a woe-begone expression that no actress would despise; And if you'd never heard it, why you would imagine surely That you'd need your pocket-handkerchief to wipe your weeping eyes.

When age my hair has silvered, and my step has grown unsteady, And the nearest to my vision are the scenes of long ago, I shall see the pretty picture, and the tears may come as ready As the laugh did, when I used to--ha! ha! ha! and--ho! ho! ho!

A SONNET.

BY JOSEPHINE POLLARD.

Once a poet wrote a sonnet All about a pretty bonnet, And a critic sat upon it (On the sonnet, Not the bonnet), Nothing loath.

And as if it were high treason, He said: "Neither rhyme nor reason Has it; and it's out of season," Which? the sonnet Or the bonnet? Maybe both.

"'Tis a feeble imitation Of a worthier creation; An aesthetic innovation!" Of a sonnet Or a bonnet? This was hard.

Both were put together neatly, Harmonizing very sweetly, But the critic crushed completely Not the bonnet, Or the sonnet, But the bard.

WANTED, A MINISTER.

BY MRS. M.E.W. SKEELS.

We've a church, tho' the belfry is leaning, They are talking I think of repair, And the bell, oh, pray but excuse us, 'Twas talked of, but never's been there. Now, "Wanted, a real live minister," And to settle the same for life, We've an organ and some one to play it, So we don't care a fig for his wife.

We once had a pastor (don't tell it), But we chanced on a time to discover That his sermons were writ long ago, And he had preached them twice over. How sad this mistake, tho' unmeaning, Oh, it made such a desperate muss! Both deacon and laymen were vexed, And decided, "He's no man for us."

And then the "old nick" was to pay, "Truth indeed is stranger than fiction," His prayers were so tedious and long, People slept, till the benediction. And then came another, on trial, Who actually preached in his gloves, His manner so awkward and queer, That we settled him off and he moved.

And then came another so meek, That his name really ought to 've been Moses; We almost considered him settled, When lo! the secret discloses, He'd attacks of nervous disease, That unfit him for every-day duty; His sermons, oh, never can please, They lack both in force and beauty.

Now, "wanted, a minister," really, That won't preach his old sermons over, That will make short prayers while in church, With no fault that the ear can discover, That is very forbearing, yes very, That blesses wherever he moves-- Not too zealous, nor lacking for zeal, That preaches without any gloves!

Now, "wanted, a minister," really, "That was born ere nerves came in fashion," That never complains of the "headache," That never is roused to a passion. He must add to the wisdom of Solomon The unwearied patience of Job, Must be mute in political matters, Or doff his clerical robe.

If he pray for the present Congress, He must speak in an undertone; If he pray for President Johnson, He NEEDS 'em, why let him go on. He must touch upon doctrines so lightly, That no one can take an offence, Mustn't meddle with predestination-- In short, must preach "common sense."

Now really wanted a minister, With religion enough to sustain him, For the salary's exceedingly small, And faith alone must maintain him. He must visit the sick and afflicted, Must mourn with those that mourn, Must preach the "funeral sermons" With a very peculiar turn.

He must preach at the north-west school-house On every Thursday eve, And things too numerous to mention He must do, and must believe. He must be of careful demeanor, Both graceful and eloquent too, Must adjust his cravat "a la mode," Wear his beaver, decidedly, so.

Now if some one will deign to be shepherd To this "our peculiar people," Will be first to subscribe for a bell, And help us to right up the steeple, If correct in doctrinal points (We've a committee of investigation), If possessed of these requisite graces, We'll accept him perhaps on probation.

Then if two-thirds of the church can agree, We'll settle him here for life; Now, we advertise, "Wanted, a Minister," And not a minister's wife.

THE MIDDY OF 1881.

BY MAY CROLY ROPER.

I'm the dearest, I'm the sweetest little mid To be found in journeying from here to Hades, I am also, nat-u-rally, a prodid- Gious favorite with all the pretty ladies. I know nothing, but say a mighty deal; My elevated nose, likewise, comes handy; I stalk around, my great importance feel-- In short, I'm a brainless little dandy.

My hair is light, and waves above my brow, My mustache can just be seen through opera-glasses; I originate but flee from every row, And no one knows as well as I what "sass" is! The officers look down on me with scorn, The sailors jeer at me--behind my jacket, But still my heart is not "with anguish torn," And life with me is one continued racket.

Whene'er the captain sends me with a boat, The seamen know an idiot has got 'em; They make their wills and are prepared to die, Quite certain they are going to the bottom. But what care I! For when I go ashore, In uniform with buttons bright and shining, The girls all cluster 'round me to adore, And lots of 'em for love of me are pining.

I strut and dance, and fool my life away; I'm nautical in past and future tenses! Long as I know an ocean from a bay, I'll shy the rest, and take the consequences. I'm the dearest, I'm the sweetest little mid That ever graced the tail-end of his classes, And through a four years' course of study slid, First am I in the list of Nature's--donkeys!

--Scribner's Magazine Bric-?Brac, 1881.

INDIGNANT POLLY WOG.

BY MARGARET EYTINGE.

A tree-toad dressed in apple-green Sat on a mossy log Beside a pond, and shrilly sang, "Come forth, my Polly Wog-- My Pol, my Ly,--my Wog, My pretty Polly Wog, I've something very sweet to say, My slender Polly Wog!

"The air is moist, the moon is hid Behind a heavy fog; No stars are out to wink and blink At you, my Polly Wog-- My Pol, my Ly--my Wog, My graceful Polly Wog; Oh, tarry not, beloved one! My precious Polly Wog!"

Just then away went clouds, and there A sitting on the log-- The other end I mean--the moon Showed angry Polly Wog.

Her small eyes flashed, she swelled until She looked almost a frog; "How dare you, sir, call me," she asked, "Your precious Polly Wog?

"Why, one would think you'd spent your life In some low, muddy bog. I'd have you know--to strange young men My name's Miss Mary Wog."

One wild, wild laugh that tree-toad gave, And tumbled off the log, And on the ground he kicked and screamed, "Oh, Mary, Mary Wog. Oh, May! oh, Ry-- oh, Wog! Oh, proud Miss Mary Wog! Oh, goodness gracious! what a joke! Hurrah for Mary Wog!"

"KISS PRETTY POLL!"

BY MARY D. BRINE.

"Kiss Pretty Poll!" the parrot screamed, And "Pretty Poll," repeated I, The while I stole a merry glance Across the room all on the sly, Where some one plied her needle fast, Demurely by the window sitting; But I beheld upon her cheek A multitude of blushes flitting.

"Kiss Pretty Poll," the parrot coaxed: "I would, but dare not try," I said, And stole another glance to see How some one drooped her golden head, And sought for something on the floor (The loss was only feigned, I knew)-- And still, "Kiss Poll," the parrot screamed, The very thing I longed to do.

But some one turned to me at last, "Please, won't you keep that parrot still?" "Why, yes," said I, "at least--you see If you will let me, dear, I will." And so--well, never mind the rest; But some one said it was a shame To take advantage just because A foolish parrot bore her name.

--Harper's Weekly.

THANKSGIVING-DAY (THEN AND NOW).

BY MARY D. BRINE.

Thanksgiving-day, a year ago, A bachelor was I, Free as the winds that whirl and blow, Or clouds that sail on high: I smoked my meerschaum blissfully, And tilted back my chair, And on the mantel placed my feet, For who would heed or care?

The fellows gathered in my room For many an hour of fun, Or I would meet them at the club For cards, till night was done. I came or went as pleased me best, Myself the first and last. One year ago! Ah, can it be That freedom's age is past?

Now, here's a note just come from Fred: "Old fellow, will you dine With me to-day? and meet the boys, A jolly number--nine?" Ah, Fred is quite as free to-day As just a year ago, And ignorant, happily, I may say, Of things I've learned to know.

I'd like, yes, if the truth were known, I'd like to join the boys, But then a Benedick must learn To cleave to other joys. So, here's my answer: "Fred, old chum, I much regret--oh, pshaw! To tell the truth, I've got to dine With--my dear mother-in-law!"

--Harper's Weekly.

CONCERNING MOSQUITOES.

Feelingly Dedicated to their Discounted Bills.

BY MISS ANNA A. GORDON.

Skeeters have the reputation Of continuous application To their poisonous profession; Never missing nightly session, Wearing out your life's existence By their practical persistence.

Would I had the power to veto Bills of every mosquito; Then I'd pass a peaceful summer, With no small nocturnal hummer Feasting on my circulation, For his regular potation.

Oh, that rascally mosquito! He's a fellow you must see to; Which you can't do if you're napping, But must evermore be slapping Quite promiscuous on your features; For you'll seldom hit the creatures.

But the thing most aggravating Is the cool and calculating Way in which he tunes his harpstring To the melody of sharp sting; Then proceeds to serenade you, And successfully evade you.

When a skeeter gets through stealing, He sails upward to the ceiling, Where he sits in deep reflection How he perched on your complexion, Filled with solid satisfaction At results of his extraction.

Would you know, in this connection, How you may secure protection For yourself and city cousins From these bites and from these buzzin's? Show your sense by quickly getting For each window--skeeter netting.

THE STILTS OF GOLD.

BY METTA VICTORIA VICTOR.

Mrs. Mackerel sat in her little room, Back of her husband's grocery store, Trying to see through the evening gloom, To finish the baby's pinafore. She stitched away with a steady hand, Though her heart was sore, to the very core, To think of the troublesome little band, (There were seven, or more), And the trousers, frocks, and aprons they wore, Made and mended by her alone. "Slave, slave!" she said, in a mournful tone; "And let us slave, and contrive, and fret, I don't suppose we shall ever get A little home which is all our own, With my own front door Apart from the store, And the smell of fish and tallow no more."

These words to herself she sadly spoke, Breaking the thread from the last-set stitch, When Mackerel into her presence broke-- "Wife, we're--we're--we're, wife, we're--we're rich!" "We rich! ha, ha! I'd like to see; I'll pull your hair if you're fooling me." "Oh, don't, love, don't! the letter is here-- You can read the news for yourself, my dear. The one who sent you that white crape shawl-- There'll be no end to our gold--he's dead; You know you always would call him stingy, Because he didn't invite us to Injy; And I am his only heir, 'tis said. A million of pounds, at the very least, And pearls and diamonds, likely, beside!" Mrs. Mackerel's spirits rose like yeast-- "How lucky I married you, Mac," she cried. Then the two broke forth into frantic glee. A customer hearing the strange commotion, Peeped into the little back-room, and he Was seized with the very natural notion That the Mackerel family had gone insane; So he ran away with might and main.

Mac shook his partner by both her hands; They dance, they giggle, they laugh, they stare; And now on his head the grocer stands, Dancing a jig with his feet in air-- Remarkable feat for a man of his age, Who never had danced upon any stage But the High-Bridge stage, when he set on top, And whose green-room had been a green-grocer's shop. But that Mrs. Mac should perform so well Is not very strange, if the tales they tell Of her youthful days have any foundation. But let that pass with her former life-- An opera-girl may make a good wife, If she happens to get such a nice situation.

A million pounds of solid gold One would have thought would have crushed them dead; But dear they bobbed, and courtesied, and rolled Like a couple of corks to a plummet of lead. 'Twas enough the soberest fancy to tickle To see the two Mackerels in such a pickle! It was three o'clock when they got to bed; Even then through Mrs. Mackerel's head Such gorgeous dreams went whirling away, "Like a Catherine-wheel," she declared next day, "That her brain seemed made of sparkles of fire Shot off in spokes, with a ruby tire."

Mrs. Mackerel had ever been One of the upward-tending kind, Regarded by husband and by kin As a female of very ambitious mind. It had fretted her long and fretted her sore To live in the rear of the grocery-store. And several times she was heard to say She would sell her soul for a year and a day To the King of Brimstone, Fire, and Pitch, For the power and pleasure of being rich.

Now her ambition had scope to work-- Riches, they say, are a burden at best; Her onerous burden she did not shirk, But carried it all with commendable zest; Leaving her husband with nothing in life But to smoke, eat, drink, and obey his wife. She built a house with a double front-door, A marble house in the modern style, With silver planks in the entry floor, And carpets of extra-magnificent pile. And in the hall, in the usual manner, "A statue," she said, "of the chased Diana; Though who it was chased her, or whether they Caught her or not, she could, really, not say." A carriage with curtains of yellow satin-- A coat-of-arms with these rare devices: "A mackerel sky and the starry Pisces--" And underneath, in the purest fish-latin, If fishibus flyabus They may reach the skyabus!

Yet it was not in common affairs like these She showed her original powers of mind; Her soul was fired, her ardor inspired, To stand apart from the rest of mankind; "To be A No. one," her husband said; At which she turned very angrily red, For she couldn't endure the remotest hint Of the grocery-store, and the mackerels in't. Weeks and months she plotted and planned To raise herself from the common level; Apart from even the few to stand Who'd hundreds of thousands on which to revel. Her genius, at last, spread forth its wings-- Stilts, golden stilts, are the very things-- "I'll walk on stilts," Mrs. Mackerel cried, In the height of her overtowering pride. Her husband timidly shook his head; But she did not care--"For why," as she said, "Should the owner of more than a million pounds Be going the rounds On the very same grounds As those low people, she couldn't tell who, They might keep a shop, for all she knew."

She had a pair of the articles made, Of solid gold, gorgeously overlaid With every color of precious stone Which ever flashed in the Indian zone. She privately practised many a day Before she ventured from home at all; She had lost her girlish skill, and they say That she suffered many a fearful fall; But pride is stubborn, and she was bound On her golden stilts to go around, Three feet, at least, from the plebeian ground. 'Twas an exquisite day, In the month of May, That the stilts came out for a promenade; Their first entree Was made on the shilling side of Broadway; The carmen whistled, the boys went mad, The omnibus-drivers their horses stopped. The chestnut-roaster his chestnuts dropped, The popper of corn no longer popped; The daintiest dandies deigned to stare, And even the heads of women fair Were turned by the vision meeting them there. The stilts they sparkled and flashed and shone Like the tremulous lights of the frigid zone, Crimson and yellow and sapphire and green, Bright as the rainbows in summer seen; While the lady she strode along between With a majesty too supremely serene For anything but an American queen. A lady with jewels superb as those, And wearing such very expensive clothes, Might certainly do whatever she chose! And thus, in despite of the jeering noise, And the frantic delight of the little boys, The stilts were a very decided success. The creme de la creme paid profoundest attention, The merchants' clerks bowed in such wild excess, When she entered their shops, that they strained their spines, And afterward went into rapid declines. The papers, next day, gave her flattering mention; "The wife of our highly-esteemed fellow-citizen, A Mackerel, of Codfish Square, in this city, Scorning French fashions, herself has hit on one So very piquant and stylish and pretty, We trust our fair friends will consider it treason Not to walk upon stilts, by the close of the season."

Mrs. Mackerel, now, was never seen Out of her chamber, day or night, Unless her stilts were along--her mien Was very imposing from such a height, It imposed upon many a dazzled wight, Who snuffed the perfume floating down From the rustling folds of her gorgeous gown, But never could smell through these bouquets The fishy odor of former days. She went on her golden stilts to pray, Which never became her better than then, When her murmuring lips were heard to say, "Thank God, I am not as my fellow-men!" Her pastor loved as a pastor might-- His house that was built on a golden rock; He pointed it out as a shining light To the lesser lambs of his fleecy flock. The stilts were a help to the church, no doubt, They kindled its self-expiring embers, So that before the season was out It gained a dozen excellent members.

Mrs. Mackerel gave a superb soiree, Standing on stilts to receive her guests; The gas-lights mimicked the glowing day So well, that the birds, in their flowery nests, Almost burst their beautiful breasts, Trilling away their musical stories In Mrs. Mackerel's conservatories. She received on stilts; a distant bow Was all the loftiest could attain-- Though some of her friends she did allow To kiss the hem of her jewelled train. One gentleman screamed himself quite hoarse Requesting her to dance; which, of course, Couldn't be done on stilts, as she Halloed down to him rather scornfully.

The fact is, when Mackerel kept a shop, His wife was very fond of a hop, And now, as the music swelled and rose, She felt a tingling in her toes, A restless, tickling, funny sensation Which didn't agree with her exaltation.

When the maddened music was at its height, And the waltz was wildest-- behold, a sight! The stilts began to hop and twirl Like the saucy feet of a ballet-girl. And their haughty owner, through the air, Was spin, spin, spinning everywhere. Everybody got out of the way To give the dangerous stilts fair play. In every corner, at every door, With faces looking like unfilled blanks, They watched the stilts at their airy pranks, Giving them, unrequested, the floor. They never had glittered so bright before; The light it flew in flashing splinters Away from those burning, revolving centres; While the gems on the lady's flying skirts Gave out their light in jets and spirts. Poor Mackerel gazed in mute dismay At this unprecedented display. "Oh, stop, love, stop!" he cried at last; But she only flew more wild and fast, While the flutes and fiddles, bugle and drum, Followed as if their time had come.

She went at such a bewildering pace Nobody saw the lady's face, But only a ring of emerald light From the crown she wore on that fatal night. Whether the stilts were propelling her, Or she the stilts, none could aver. Around and around the magnificent hall Mrs. Mackerel danced at her own grand ball.

"As the twig is bent the tree's inclined;" This must have been a case in kind. "What's in the blood will sometimes show--" 'Round and around the wild stilts go.

It had been whispered many a time That when poor Mack was in his prime Keeping that little retail store, He had fallen in love with a ballet-girl, Who gave up fame's entrancing whirl To be his own, and the world's no more. She made him a faithful, prudent wife-- Ambitious, however, all her life. Could it be that the soft, alluring waltz Had carried her back to a former age, Making her memory play her false, Till she dreamed herself on the gaudy stage? Her crown a tinsel crown--her guests The pit that gazes with praise and jests?

"Pride," they say, "must have a fall--" Mrs. Mackerel was very proud-- And now she danced at her own grand ball, While the music swelled more fast and loud.

The gazers shuddered with mute affright, For the stilts burned now with a bluish light, While a glimmering, phosphorescent glow Did out of the lady's garments flow. And what was that very peculiar smell? Fish, or brimstone? no one could tell. Stronger and stronger the odor grew, And the stilts and the lady burned more blue; 'Round and around the long saloon, While Mackerel gazed in a partial swoon, She approached the throng, or circled from it, With a flaming train like the last great comet; Till at length the crowd All groaned aloud. For her exit she made from her own grand ball Out of the window, stilts and all.

None of the guests can really say How she looked when she vanished away. Some declare that she carried sail On a flying fish with a lambent tail; And some are sure she went out of the room Riding her stilts like a witch a broom, While a phosphorent odor followed her track: Be this as it may, she never came back. Since then, her friends of the gold-fish fry Are in a state of unpleasant suspense, Afraid, that unless they unselfishly try To make better use of their dollars and sense To chasten their pride, and their manners mend, They may meet a similar shocking end.

--Cosmopolitan Art Journal.

JUST SO.

BY METTA VICTORIA VICTOR.

A youth and maid, one winter night, Were sitting in the corner; His name, we're told, was Joshua White, And hers was Patience Warner.

Not much the pretty maiden said, Beside the young man sitting; Her cheeks were flushed a rosy red, Her eyes bent on her knitting.

Nor could he guess what thoughts of him Were to her bosom flocking, As her fair fingers, swift and slim, Flew round and round the stocking.

While, as for Joshua, bashful youth, His words grew few and fewer; Though all the time, to tell the truth, His chair edged nearer to her.

Meantime her ball of yarn gave out, She knit so fast and steady; And he must give his aid, no doubt, To get another ready.

He held the skein; of course the thread Got tangled, snarled and twisted; "Have Patience!" cried the artless maid, To him who her assisted.

Good chance was this for tongue-tied churl To shorten all palaver; "Have Patience!" cried he, "dearest girl! And may I really have her?"

The deed was done; no more, that night, Clicked needles in the corner:-- And she is Mrs. Joshua White That once was Patience Warner.

THE INVENTOR'S WIFE.

BY E.T. CORBETT.

It's easy to talk of the patience of Job. Humph! Job had nothin' to try him; Ef he'd been married to 'Bijah Brown, folks wouldn't have dared come nigh him. Trials, indeed! Now I'll tell you what--ef you want to be sick of your life, Jest come and change places with me a spell, for I'm an inventor's wife. And sech inventions! I'm never sure when I take up my coffee-pot, That 'Bijah hain't been "improvin'" it, and it mayn't go off like a shot. Why, didn't he make me a cradle once that would keep itself a-rockin', And didn't it pitch the baby out, and wasn't his head bruised shockin'? And there was his "patent peeler," too, a wonderful thing I'll say; But it hed one fault--it never stopped till the apple was peeled away. As for locks and clocks, and mowin' machines, and reapers, and all such trash, Why, 'Bijah's invented heaps of them, but they don't bring in no cash! Law! that don't worry him--not at all; he's the aggravatinest man-- He'll set in his little workshop there, and whistle and think and plan, Inventin' a Jews harp to go by steam, or a new-fangled powder-horn, While the children's goin' barefoot to school, and the weeds is chokin' our corn. When 'Bijah and me kep' company, he wasn't like this, you know; Our folks all thought he was dreadful smart--but that was years ago. He was handsome as any pictur' then, and he had such a glib, bright way-- I never thought that a time would come when I'd rue my weddin'-day; But when I've been forced to chop the wood, and tend to the farm beside, And look at 'Bijah a-settin' there, I've jest dropped down and cried. We lost the hull of our turnip crop while he was inventin' a gun, But I counted it one of my marcies when it bust before 'twas done. So he turned it into a "burglar alarm." It ought to give thieves a fright-- 'Twould scare an honest man out of his wits, ef he sot it off at night. Sometimes I wonder ef 'Bijah's crazy, he does such curious things. Have I told you about his bedstead yit? 'Twas full of wheels and springs; It hed a key to wind it up, and a clock-face at the head; All you did was to turn them hands, and at any hour you said That bed got up and shook itself, and bounced you on the floor, And then shet up, jest like a box, so you couldn't sleep any more. Wa'al, 'Bijah he fixed it all complete, and he sot it at half-past five, But he hadn't more 'n got into it, when--dear me! sakes alive! Them wheels began to whizz and whirr! I heard a fearful snap, And there was that bedstead with 'Bijah inside shet up jest like a trap! I screamed, of course, but 'twant no use. Then I worked that hull long night A-tryin' to open the pesky thing. At last I got in a fright: I couldn't hear his voice inside, and I thought he might be dyin', So I took a crowbar and smashed it in. There was 'Bijah peacefully lyin', Inventin' a way to git out agin. That was all very well to say, But I don't believe he'd have found it out if I'd left him in all day. Now, since I've told you my story, do you wonder I'm tired of life, Or think it strange I often wish I warn't an inventor's wife?

AN UNRUFFLED BOSOM.

(Story of an old Woman who knew Washington.)

BY LIZZIE W. CHAMPNEY.

An aged negress at her door Is sitting in the sun; Her day of work is almost o'er, Her day of rest begun. Her face is black as darkest night, Her form is bent and thin, And o'er her bony visage tight Is stretched her wrinkled skin. Her dress is scant and mean; yet still About her ebon face There flows a soft and creamy frill Of costly Mechlin lace. What means the contrast strange and wide? Its like is seldom seen-- A pauper's aged face beside The laces of a queen. Her mien is stately, proud, and high, And yet her look is kind, And the calm light within her eye Speaks an unruffled mind. "Dar comes anodder ob dem tramps," She mumbles low in wrath, "I know dose sleek Centennial chaps Quick as dey mounts de path." A-axing ob a lady's age I tink is impolite, And when dey gins to interview I disremembers quite. Dar was dat spruce photometer Dat tried to take my head, And Mr. Squibbs, de porterer, Wrote down each word I said. Six hundred years I t'ought it was, Or else it was sixteen-- Yes; I'd shook hands wid Washington And likewise General Greene. I tole him all de generals' names Dar ebber was, I guess, From General Lee and La Fayette To General Distress. Den dar's dem high-flown ladies My old tings came to see; Wanted to buy dem some heirlooms Of real Aunt Tiquity. Says I, "Dat isn't dis chile's name, Dey calls me Auntie Scraggs," And den I axed dem, by de pound How much dey gabe for rags? De missionary had de mose Insurance of dem all; He tole me I was ole, and said, Leabes had dar time to fall. He simply wished to ax, he said, As pastor and as friend, If wid unruffled bosom I Approached my latter end. Now how he knew dat story I Should mightily like to know.

I 'clar to goodness, Massa Guy, If dat ain't really you! You say dat in your wash I sent You only one white vest; And as you'se passin' by you t'ought You'd call and get de rest. Now, Massa Guy, about your shirts, At least, it seems to me Dat you is more particular Dan what you used to be. Your family pride is stiff as starch, Your blood is mighty blue-- I nebber spares de indigo To make your shirts so, too. I uses candle ends, and wax, And satin-gloss and paints, Until your wristbands shine like to De pathway ob de saints. But when a gemman sends to me Eight white vests eberry week, A stain ob har-oil on each one, I tinks it's time to speak.

When snarled around a button dar's A golden har or so, Dat young man's going to be wed, Or someting's wrong, I know. You needn't laugh, and turn it off By axing 'bout my cap; You didn't use to know nice lace, And never cared a snap What 'twas a lady wore. But folks Wid teaching learn a lot, And dey do say Miss Bella buys De best dat's to be got. But if you really want to know, I don't mind telling you Jus' how I come by dis yere lace-- It's cur'us, but it's true. My mother washed for Washington When I warn't more'n dat tall; I cut one of his shirt-frills off To dress my corn-cob doll; And when de General saw de shirt, He jus' was mad enough To tink he got to hold review Widout his best Dutch ruff. Ma'am said she 'lowed it was de calf Dat had done chawed it off; But when de General heard dat ar, He answered with a scoff; He said de marks warn't don' of teef, But plainly dose ob shears; An' den he showed her to de do' And cuffed me on ye years. And when my ma'am arribed at home She stretched me 'cross her lap, Den took de lace away from me An' sewed it on her cap. And when I dies I hope dat dey Wid it my shroud will trim.

Den when we meets on Judgment Day, I'll gib it back to him. So dat's my story, Massa Guy, Maybe I's little wit; But I has larned to, when I'm wrong, Make a clean breast ob it. Den keep a conscience smooth and white (You can't if much you flirt), And an unruffled bosom, like De General's Sunday shirt.

HAT, ULSTER AND ALL.

BY CHARLOTTE FISKE BATES.

John Verity's Experience.

I saw the congregation rise, And in it, to my great surprise, A Kossuth-covered head. I looked and looked, and looked again, To make quite sure my sight was plain, Then to myself I said:

That fellow surely is a Jew, To whom the Christian faith is new, Nor is it strange, indeed, If used to wear his hat in church, His manners leave him in the lurch Upon a change of creed.

Joining my friend on going out, Conjecture soon was put to rout By smothered laugh of his: Ha! ha! too good, too good, no Jew, Dear fellow, but Miss Moll Carew, Good Christian that she is!

Bad blunder all I have to say, It is a most unchristian way To rig Miss Moll Carew-- She has my hat, my cut of hair, Just such an ulster as I wear, And heaven knows what else, too.

AUCTION EXTRAORDINARY.

BY LUCRETIA DAVIDSON.

I dreamed a dream in the midst of my slumbers, And as fast as I dreamed it, it came into numbers; My thoughts ran along in such beautiful meter, I'm sure I ne'er saw any poetry sweeter: It seemed that a law had been recently made That a tax on old bachelors' pates should be laid; And in order to make them all willing to marry, The tax was as large as a man could well carry. The bachelors grumbled and said 'twas no use-- 'Twas horrid injustice and horrid abuse, And declared that to save their own hearts' blood from spilling, Of such a vile tax they would not pay a shilling. But the rulers determined them still to pursue, So they set all the old bachelors up at vendue: A crier was sent through the town to and fro, To rattle his bell and a trumpet to blow, And to call out to all he might meet in his way, "Ho! forty old bachelors sold here to-day!" And presently all the old maids in the town, Each in her very best bonnet and gown, From thirty to sixty, fair, plain, red and pale, Of every description, all flocked to the sale. The auctioneer then in his labor began, And called out aloud, as he held up a man, "How much for a bachelor? Who wants to buy?" In a twink, every maiden responsed, "I--I!" In short, at a highly extravagant price, The bachelors all were sold off in a trice: And forty old maidens, some younger, some older, Each lugged an old bachelor home on her shoulder.

A APELE FOR ARE TO THE SEXTANT.

BY ARABELLA WILSON.

O Sextant of the meetinouse which sweeps And dusts, or is supposed to! and makes fiers, And lites the gas, and sumtimes leaves a screw loose, In which case it smells orful--wus than lampile; And wrings the Bel and toles it when men dies To the grief of survivin' pardners, and sweeps paths, And for these servaces gits $100 per annum; Wich them that thinks deer let 'em try it; Gittin up before starlite in all wethers, and Kindlin' fiers when the wether is as cold As zero, and like as not green wood for kindlins (I wouldn't be hierd to do it for no sum); But o Sextant there are one kermodity Wuth more than gold which don't cost nuthin; Wuth more than anything except the Sole of man! I mean pewer Are, Sextant, I mean pewer Are! O it is plenty out o' dores, so plenty it doant no What on airth to do with itself, but flize about Scatterin leaves and bloin off men's hats; In short its jest as free as Are out dores; But O Sextant! in our church its scarce as piety, Scarce as bankbills when ajunts beg for mishuns, Which sum say is purty often, taint nuthin to me, What I give aint nuthing to nobody; but O Sextant! You shet 500 men women and children Speshily the latter, up in a tite place, Sum has bad breths, none of em aint too sweet, Sum is fevery, sum is scroflus, sum has bad teeth And sum haint none, and sum aint over clean; But evry one of em brethes in and out and in Say 50 times a minnet, or 1 million and a half breths an hour; Now how long will a church full of are last at that rate? I ask you; say fifteen minnets, and then what's to be did? Why then they must breth it all over agin, And then agin and so on, till each has took it down At least ten times and let it up agin, and what's more, The same individible doant have the privilege Of breathin his own are and no one else, Each one must take wotever comes to him, O Sextant! doant you know our lungs is belluses To blo the fier of life and keep it from Going out: und how can bellusses blo without wind? And aint wind are? I put it to your konshens, Are is the same to us as milk to babies, Or water is to fish, or pendlums to clox, Or roots and airbs unto an Injun doctor, Or little pills unto an omepath, Or Boze to girls. Are is for us to brethe. What signifize who preaches ef I cant brethe? What's Pol? What's Pollus to sinners who are ded? Ded for want of breth! Why Sextant when we dye Its only coz we cant brethe no more--that's all. And now O Sextant? let me beg of you To let a little are into our cherch (Pewer are is sertin proper for the pews); And dew it week days and on Sundays tew-- It aint much trobble-- only make a hoal, And then the are will come in of itself (It love to come in where it can git warm). And O how it will rouze the people up And sperrit up the preacher, and stop garps And yorns and fijits as effectool As wind on the dry boans the Profit tels of.

--Christian Weekly.

CHAPTER IX.

GOOD-NATURED SATIRE.

Women show their sense of humor in ridiculing the foibles of their own sex, as Miss Carlotta Perry seeing the danger of "higher education," and Helen Gray Cone laughing over the exaggerated ravings and moanings of a stage-struck girl, or the very one-sided sermon of a sentimental goose.

A MODERN MINERVA.

BY CARLOTTA PERRY.

'Twas the height of the gay season, and I cannot tell the reason, But at a dinner party given by Mrs. Major Thwing It became my pleasant duty to take out a famous beauty-- The prettiest woman present. I was happy as a king.

Her dress beyond a question was an artist's best creation; A miracle of loveliness was she from crown to toe. Her smile was sweet as could be, her voice just as it should be-- Not high, and sharp, and wiry, but musical and low.

Her hair was soft and flossy, golden, plentiful and glossy; Her eyes, so blue and sunny, shone with every inward grace; I could see that every fellow in the room was really yellow With jealousy, and wished himself that moment in my place.

As the turtle soup we tasted, like a gallant man I hasted To pay some pretty tribute to this muslin, silk, and gauze; But she turned and softly asked me-- and I own the question tasked me-- What were my fixed opinions on the present Suffrage laws.

I admired a lovely blossom resting on her gentle bosom; The remark I thought a safe one--I could hardly made a worse; With a smile like any Venus, she gave me its name and genus, And opened very calmly a botanical discourse.

But I speedily recovered. As her taper fingers hovered, Like a tender benediction, in a little bit of fish, Further to impair digestion, she brought up the Eastern Question. By that time I fully echoed that other fellow's wish.

And, as sure as I'm a sinner, right on through that endless dinner Did she talk of moral science, of politics and law, Of natural selection, of Free Trade and Protection, Till I came to look upon her with a sort of solemn awe.

Just to hear the lovely woman, looking more divine than human, Talk with such discrimination of Ingersoll and Cook, With such a childish, sweet smile, quoting Huxley, Mill, and Carlyle-- It was quite a revelation--it was better than a book.

Chemistry and mathematics, agriculture and chromatics, Music, painting, sculpture--she knew all the tricks of speech; Bas-relief and chiaroscuro, and at last the Indian Bureau-- She discussed it quite serenely, as she trifled with a peach.

I have seen some dreadful creatures, with vinegary features, With their fearful store of learning set me sadly in eclipse; But I'm ready quite to swear if I have ever heard the Tariff Or the Eastern Question settled by such a pair of lips.

Never saw I a dainty maiden so remarkably o'erladen From lip to tip of finger with the love of books and men; Quite in confidence I say it, and I trust you'll not betray it, But I pray to gracious heaven that I never may again.

--Chicago Tribune.

THE BALLAD OF CASSANDRA BROWN.

BY HELEN GRAY CONE.

Though I met her in the summer, when one's heart lies 'round at ease, As it were in tennis costume, and a man's not hard to please; Yet I think at any season to have met her was to love, While her tones, unspoiled, unstudied, had the softness of the dove.

At request she read us poems, in a nook among the pines, And her artless voice lent music to the least melodious lines; Though she lowered her shadowing lashes, in an earnest reader's wise, Yet we caught blue gracious glimpses of the heavens that were her eyes.

As in Paradise I listened. Ah, I did not understand That a little cloud, no larger than the average human hand, Might, as stated oft in fiction, spread into a sable pall, When she said that she should study elocution in the fall.

I admit her earliest efforts were not in the Ercles vein: She began with "Little Maaybel, with her faayce against the paayne, And the beacon-light a-trrremble--" which, although it made me wince, Is a thing of cheerful nature to the things she's rendered since.

Having learned the Soulful Quiver, she acquired the Melting Mo-o-an, And the way she gave "Young Grayhead" would have liquefied a stone; Then the Sanguinary Tragic did her energies employ, And she tore my taste to tatters when she slew "The Polish Boy."

It's not pleasant for a fellow when the jewel of his soul Wades through slaughter on the carpet, while her orbs in frenzy roll: What was I that I should murmur? Yet it gave me grievous pain When she rose in social gatherings and searched among the slain.

I was forced to look upon her, in my desperation dumb-- Knowing well that when her awful opportunity was come She would give us battle, murder, sudden death at very least-- As a skeleton of warning, and a blight upon the feast.

Once, ah! once I fell a-dreaming; some one played a polonaise I associated strongly with those happier August days; And I mused, "I'll speak this evening," recent pangs forgotten quite. Sudden shrilled a scream of anguish: "Curfew SHALL not ring to-night!"

Ah, that sound was as a curfew, quenching rosy warm romance! Were it safe to wed a woman one so oft would wish in France? Oh, as she "cull-imbed!" that ladder, swift my mounting hope came down. I am still a single cynic; she is still Cassandra Brown!

THE TENDER HEART.

BY HELEN GRAY CONE.

She gazed upon the burnished brace Of plump, ruffed grouse he showed with pride, Angelic grief was in her face: "How could you do it, dear?" she sighed. "The poor, pathetic moveless wings!" The songs all hushed--"Oh, cruel shame!" Said he, "The partridge never sings," Said she, "The sin is quite the same."

"You men are savage, through and through, A boy is always bringing in Some string of birds' eggs, white and blue, Or butterfly upon a pin. The angle-worm in anguish dies, Impaled, the pretty trout to tease--" "My own, we fish for trout with flies--" "Don't wander from the question, please."

She quoted Burns's "Wounded Hare," And certain burning lines of Blake's, And Ruskin on the fowls of air, And Coleridge on the water-snakes. At Emerson's "Forbearance" he Began to feel his will benumbed; At Browning's "Donald" utterly His soul surrendered and succumbed.

"Oh, gentlest of all gentle girls! He thought, beneath the blessed sun!" He saw her lashes hang with pearls, And swore to give away his gun. She smiled to find her point was gained And went, with happy parting words (He subsequently ascertained), To trim her hat with humming birds.

--From the Century.

A dozen others equally good must be reserved for that encyclopedia! This specimen, of vers de society rivals Locker or Baker:

PLIGHTED: A.D. 1874.

BY ALICE WILLIAMS.

"Two souls with but a single thought, Two hearts that beat as one."

NELLIE, loquitur.

Bless my heart! You've come at last, Awful glad to see you, dear! Thought you'd died or something, Belle-- Such an age since you've been here! My engagement? Gracious! Yes. Rumor's hit the mark this time. And the victim? Charley Gray. Know him, don't you? Well, he's prime. Such mustachios! splendid style! Then he's not so horrid fast-- Waltzes like a seraph, too; Has some fortune--best and last. Love him? Nonsense. Don't be "soft;" Pretty much as love now goes; He's devoted, and in time I'll get used to him, I 'spose. First love? Humbug. Don't talk stuff! Bella Brown, don't be a fool! Next you'd rave of flames and darts, Like a chit at boarding-school; Don't be "miffed." I talked just so Some two years back. Fact, my dear! But two seasons kill romance, Leave one's views of life quite clear. Why, if Will Latrobe had asked When he left two years ago, I'd have thrown up all and gone Out to Kansas, do you know? Fancy me a settler's wife! Blest escape, dear, was it not? Yes; it's hardly in my line To enact "Love in a Cot." Well, you see, I'd had my swing, Been engaged to eight or ten, Got to stop some time, of course, So it don't much matter when. Auntie hates old maids, and thinks Every girl should marry young-- On that theme my whole life long I have heard the changes sung. So, ma belle, what could I do? Charley wants a stylish wife. We'll suit well enough, no fear, When we settle down for life. But for love-stuff! See my ring! Lovely, isn't it? Solitaire. Nearly made Maud Hinton turn Green with envy and despair. Her's ain't half so nice, you see. Did I write you, Belle, about How she tried for Charley, till I sailed in and cut her out? Now, she's taken Jack McBride, I believe it's all from pique-- Threw him over once, you know-- Hates me so she'll scarcely speak. Oh, yes! Grace Church, Brown, and that-- Pa won't mind expense at last I'll be off his hands for good; Cost a fortune two years past. My trousseau shall outdo Maud's, I've carte blanche from Pa, you know-- Mean to have my dress from Worth! Won't she be just RAVING though!

--Scribner's Monthly Magazine, 1874.

* * * * *

Women are often extremely humorous in their newspaper letters, excelling in that department. As critics they incline to satire. No one who read them at the time will ever forget Mrs. Runkle's review of "St. Elmo," or Gail Hamilton's criticism of "The Story of Avis," while Mrs. Rollins, in the Critic, often uses a scimitar instead of a quill, though a smile always tempers the severity. She thus beheads a poetaster who tells the public that his "solemn song" is

"Attempt ambitious, with a ray of hope To pierce the dark abysms of thought, to guide Its dim ghosts o'er the towering crags of Doubt Unto the land where Peace and Love abide, Of flowers and streams, and sun and stars."

"His 'solemn song' is certainly very solemn for a song with so cheerful a purpose. We have rarely read, indeed, a book with so large a proportion of unhappy words in it. Frozen shrouds, souls a-chill with agony, things wan and gray, icy demons, scourging willow-branches, snow-heaped mounds, black and freezing nights, cups of sorrow drained to the lees, etc., are presented in such profusion that to struggle through the 'dark abyss' in search of the 'ray of hope' is much like taking a cup of poison to learn the sweetness of its antidote. Mr. ---- in one of his stanzas invites his soul to 'come and walk abroad' with him. If he ever found it possible to walk abroad without his soul, the fact would have been worth chronicling; but if it is true that he only desires to have his soul with him occasionally, we should advise him to walk abroad alone, and invite his soul to sit beside him in the hours he devotes to composition."

Then humor is displayed in the excellent parodies by women--as Grace Greenwood's imitations of various authors, written in her young days, but quite equal to the "Echo Club" of Bayard Taylor. How perfect her mimicry of Mrs. Sigourney!

A FRAGMENT.

BY L.H.S.

How hardly doth the cold and careless world Requite the toil divine of genius-souls, Their wasting cares and agonizing throes! I had a friend, a sweet and precious friend, One passing rich in all the strange and rare, And fearful gifts of song. On one great work, A poem in twelve cantos, she had toiled From early girlhood, e'en till she became An olden maid. Worn with intensest thought, She sunk at last, just at the "finis" sunk! And closed her eyes forever!

The soul-gem Had fretted through its casket! As I stood Beside her tomb, I made a solemn vow To take in charge that poor, lone orphan work, And edit it! My publisher I sought, A learned man and good. He took the work, Read here and there a line, then laid it down, And said, "It would not pay." I slowly turned, And went my way with troubled brow, "but more In sorrow than in anger."

* * * * *

Phoebe Cary's parody on "Maud Muller" I never fancied; it seems almost wicked to burlesque anything so perfect. But so many parodies have been made on Kingsley's "Three Fishers" that now I can enjoy a really good one, like this from Miss Lilian Whiting, of the Boston Daily Traveller, the well-known correspondent of various Western papers:

THE THREE POETS.

After Kingsley.

BY LILIAN WHITING.

Three poets went sailing down Boston streets, All into the East as the sun went down, Each felt that the editor loved him best And would welcome spring poetry in Boston town. For poets must write tho' the editors frown, Their natures will not be put down, While the harbor bar is moaning!

Three editors climbed to the highest tower That they could find in all Boston town, And they planned to conceal themselves, hour after hour, Till the sun or the poets had both gone down. For Spring poets must write, though the editors rage, The artistic spirit must thus be engaged-- Though the editors all were groaning.

Three corpses lay out on the Back Bay sand, Just after the first spring sun went down, And the Press sat down to a banquet grand, In honor of poets no more in the town. For poets will write while editors sleep, Though they've nothing to earn and no one to keep; And the harbor bar keeps moaning.

* * * * *

The humor of women is constantly seen in their poems for children, such as "The Dead Doll," by Margaret Vandergrift, and the "Motherless Turkeys," by Marian Douglas. Here are some less known:

BEDTIME.

BY NELLIE K. KELLOGG.

'Twas sunset-time, when grandma called To lively little Fred: "Come, dearie, put your toys away, It's time to go to bed."

But Fred demurred. "He wasn't tired, He didn't think 'twas right That he should go so early, when Some folks sat up all night."

Then grandma said, in pleading tone, "The little chickens go To bed at sunset ev'ry night, All summer long, you know."

Then Freddie laughed, and turned to her His eyes of roguish blue, "Oh, yes, I know," he said; "but then, Old hen goes with them, too."

--Good Cheer.

THE ROBIN AND THE CHICKEN.

BY GRACE F. COOLIDGE.

A plump little robin flew down from a tree, To hunt for a worm, which he happened to see; A frisky young chicken came scampering by, And gazed at the robin with wondering eye.

Said the chick, "What a queer-looking chicken is that! Its wings are so long and its body so fat!" While the robin remarked, loud enough to be heard: "Dear me! an exceedingly strange-looking bird!"

"Can you sing?" robin asked, and the chicken said "No;" But asked in its turn if the robin could crow. So the bird sought a tree and the chicken a wall, And each thought the other knew nothing at all.

--St. Nicholas.

* * * * *

Harriette W. Lothrop, wife of the popular publisher--better known by her pen name of "Margaret Sidney"--has done much in a humorous way to amuse and instruct little folks. She has much quiet humor.

WHY POLLY DOESN'T LOVE CAKE!

BY MARGARET SIDNEY.

They all said "No!" As they stood in a row, The poodle, and the parrot, and the little yellow cat, And they looked very solemn, This straight, indignant column, And rolled their eyes, and shook their heads, a-standing on the mat.

Then I took a goodly stick, Very short and very thick, And I said, "Dear friends, you really now shall rue it, For one of you did take That bit of wedding-cake, And so I'm going to whip you all. I honestly will do it."

Then Polly raised her claw! "I never, never saw That stuff. I'd rather have a cracker, And so it would be folly," Said this naughty, naughty Polly, "To punish me; but Pussy, you can whack her."

The cat rolled up her eyes In innocent surprise, And waved each trembling whisker end. "A crumb I have not taken, But Bose ought to be shaken. And then, perhaps, his thieving, awful ways he'll mend."

"I'll begin right here With you, Polly, dear," And my stick I raised with righteous good intent. "Oh, dear!" and "Oh, dear!" The groans that filled my ear. As over head and heels the frightened column went!

The cat flew out of window, The dog flew under bed, And Polly flapped and beat the air, Then settled on my head; When underneath her wing, From feathered corner deep, A bit of wedding-cake fell down, That made poor Polly weep.

The cat raced off to cat-land, and was never seen again, And the dog sneaked out beneath the bed to scud with might and main; While Polly sits upon her roost, and rolls her eyes in fear, And when she sees a bit of cake, she always says, "Oh, dear!"

KITTEN TACTICS.

BY ADELAIDE CILLEY WALDRON.

Four little kittens in a heap, One wide awake and three asleep. Open-eyes crowded, pushed the rest over, While the gray mother-cat went playing rover.

Three little kittens stretched and mewed; Cried out, "Open-eyes, you're too rude!" Open-eyes, winking, purred so demurely, All the rest stared at him, thinking "surely

We were the ones that were so rude, We were the ones that cried and mewed; Let us lie here like good little kittens; We cannot sleep, so we'll wash our mittens."

Four little kittens, very sleek, Purred so demurely, looked so meek, When the gray mother came home from roving-- "What good kittens!" said she; "and how loving!"

BOTH SIDES.

BY GAIL HAMILTON.

"Kitty, Kitty, you mischievous elf, What have you, pray, to say for yourself?"

But Kitty was now Asleep on the mow, And only drawled dreamily, "Ma-e-ow!"

"Kitty, Kitty, come here to me,-- The naughtiest Kitty I ever did see! I know very well what you've been about; Don't try to conceal it, murder will out. Why do you lie so lazily there?"

"Oh, I have had a breakfast rare!" "Why don't you go and hunt for a mouse?" "Oh, there's nothing fit to eat in the house."

"Dear me! Miss Kitty, This is a pity; But I guess the cause of your change of ditty. What has become of the beautiful thrush That built her nest in the heap of brush? A brace of young robins as good as the best; A round little, brown little, snug little nest; Four little eggs all green and gay, Four little birds all bare and gray, And Papa Robin went foraging round, Aloft on the trees, and alight on the ground. North wind or south wind, he cared not a groat, So he popped a fat worm down each wide-open throat; And Mamma Robin through sun and storm Hugged them up close, and kept them all warm; And me, I watched the dear little things Till the feathers pricked out on their pretty wings, And their eyes peeped up o'er the rim of the nest. Kitty, Kitty, you know the rest. The nest is empty, and silent and lone; Where are the four little robins gone? Oh, puss, you have done a cruel deed! Your eyes, do they weep? your heart, does it bleed? Do you not feel your bold cheeks turning pale? Not you! you are chasing your wicked tail. Or you just cuddle down in the hay and purr, Curl up in a ball, and refuse to stir, But you need not try to look good and wise: I see little robins, old puss, in your eyes. And this morning, just as the clock struck four, There was some one opening the kitchen door, And caught you creeping the wood-pile over,-- Make a clean breast of it, Kitty Clover!"

Then Kitty arose, Rubbed up her nose, And looked very much as if coming to blows; Rounded her back, Leaped from the stack, On her feet, at my feet, came down with a whack, Then, fairly awake, she stretched out her paws, Smoothed down her whiskers, and unsheathed her claws, Winked her green eyes With an air of surprise, And spoke rather plainly for one of her size.

"Killed a few robins; well, what of that? What's virtue in man can't be vice in a cat. There's a thing or two I should like to know,-- Who killed the chicken a week ago, For nothing at all that I could spy, But to make an overgrown chicken-pie? 'Twixt you and me, 'Tis plain to see, The odds is, you like fricassee, While my brave maw Owns no such law, Content with viands a la raw.

"Who killed the robins? Oh, yes! oh, yes! I would get the cat now into a mess! Who was it put An old stocking-foot, Tied up with strings And such shabby things, On to the end of a sharp, slender pole, Dipped it in oil and set fire to the whole, And burnt all the way from here to the miller's The nests of the sweet young caterpillars? Grilled fowl, indeed! Why, as I read, You had not even the plea of need; For all you boast Such wholesome roast, I saw no sign at tea or roast, Of even a caterpillar's ghost.

"Who killed the robins? Well, I should think! Hadn't somebody better wink At my peccadillos, if houses of glass Won't do to throw stones from at those who pass? I had four little kittens a month ago-- Black, and Malta, and white as snow; And not a very long while before I could have shown you three kittens more. And so in batches of fours and threes, Looking back as long as you please, You would find, if you read my story all, There were kittens from time immemorial.

"But what am I now? A cat bereft, Of all my kittens, but one is left. I make no charges, but this I ask,-- What made such a splurge in the waste-water cask? You are quite tender-hearted. Oh, not a doubt! But only suppose old Black Pond could speak out. Oh, bother! don't mutter excuses to me: Qui facit per alium facit per se."

"Well, Kitty, I think full enough has been said, And the best thing for you is go straight back to bed. A very fine pass Things have come to, my lass, If men must be meek While pussy-cats speak Great moral reflections in Latin and Greek!"

--Our Young Folks.

CHAPTER X.

PARODIES--REVIEWS--CHILDREN'S POEMS--COMEDIES BY WOMEN--A DRAMATIC TRIFLE--A STRING OF FIRECRACKERS.

It is surprising that we have so few comedies from women. Dr. Doran mentions five Englishwomen who wrote successful comedies. Of these, three are now forgotten; one, Aphra Behn, is remembered only to be despised for her vulgarity. She was an undoubted wit, and was never dull, but so wicked and coarse that she forfeited all right to fame.

Susanna Centlivre left nineteen plays full of vivacity and fun and lively incident. The Bold Stroke for a Wife is now considered her best. The Basset Table is also a superior comedy, especially interesting because it anticipates the modern blue-stocking in Valeria, a philosophical girl who supports vivisection, and has also a prophecy of exclusive colleges for women.

There is nothing worthy of quotation in any of these comedies. Some sentences from Mrs. Centlivre's plays are given in magazine articles to prove her wit, but we say so much brighter things in these days that they must be considered stale platitudes, as:

"You may cheat widows, orphans, and tradesmen without a blush, but a debt of honor, sir, must be paid."

"Quarrels, like mushrooms, spring up in a moment."

"Woman is the greatest sovereign power in the world."

Hans Andersen in his Autobiography mentions a Madame von Weissenthurn, who was a successful actress and dramatist. Her comedies are published in fourteen volumes. In our country several comedies written by women, but published anonymously, have been decided hits. Mrs. Verplanck's Sealed Instructions was a marked success, and years ago Fashion, by Anna Cora Mowatt, had a remarkable run. By the way, those roaring farces, Belles of the Kitchen and Fun in a Fog, were written for the Vokes family by an aunt of theirs. And I must not forget to state that Gilbert's Palace of Truth was cribbed almost bodily from Madame de Genlis's "Tales of an Old Castle." Mrs. Julia Schayer, of Washington, has given us a domestic drama in one act, entitled Struggling Genius.

STRUGGLING GENIUS.

Dramatis Person?

MRS. ANASTASIUS. GIRL OF TEN YEARS. GIRL OF TWO YEARS. MR. ANASTASIUS. GIRL OF EIGHT YEARS. INFANT OF THREE MONTHS.

ACT I.

SCENE I. NURSERY.

[Time, eight o'clock A.M. In the background nurse making bed, etc.; Girl of Two amusing herself surreptitiously with pins, buttons, scissors, etc.; Girl of Eight practising piano in adjoining room; Mrs. A. in foreground performing toilet of infant. Having lain awake half the preceding night wrestling with the plot of a new novel for which rival publishers are waiting with outstretched hands (full of checks), Mrs. A. believes she has hit upon an effective scene, and burns to commit it to paper. Washes infant with feverish haste.]

Mrs. A. (soliloquizing). Let me see! How was it? Oh! "Olga raised her eyes with a sweetly serious expression. Harold gazed moodily at her calm face. It was not the expression that he longed to see there. He would have preferred to see--" Good gracious, Maria! That child's mouth is full of buttons! "He would have preferred--preferred--" (Loudly.) Leonora! That F's to be sharped! There, there, mother's sonny boy! Did mamma drop the soap into his mouth instead of the wash-bowl? There, there! (Sings.) "There's a land that is fairer than this," etc.

[Infant quiet.

Mrs. A. (resuming). "He would have preferred--preferred--" Maria, don't you see that child has got the scissors? "He would have--" There now, let mamma put on its little socks. Now it's all dressed so nice and clean. Don'ty ky! No, don'ty! Leonora! Put more accent on the first beat. "Harold gazed moodily into--" His bottle, Maria! Quick! He'll scream himself into fits!

[Exit nurse. Baby having got both fists into his mouth beguiles himself into quiet.

Mrs. A. Let me see! How was it? Oh! "Harold gazed moodily into her calm, sweet face. It was not the expression he would have liked to find there. He would have preferred--" (Shriek from girl of two.) Oh, dear me! She has shut her darling fingers in the drawer! Come to mamma, precious love, and sit on mamma's lap, and we'll sing about little pussy.

Enter nurse with bottle. Curtain falls.

SCENE II. STUDY.

[Three hours later; infant and Girl of Two asleep; house in order; lunch and dinner arranged; buttons sewed on Girl of Eight's boots, string on Girl of Ten's hood, and both dispatched to school, etc. Enter Mrs. A. Draws a long sigh of relief and seats herself at desk. Reads a page of Dickens and a poem or two to attune herself for work. Seizes pen, scribbles erratically a few seconds and begins to write.]

Mrs. A. (after some moments). I think that is good. Let us hear how it reads. (Reads aloud.) "He would have preferred to find more passion in those deep, dark eyes. Had he then no part in the maiden meditations of this fair, innocent girl--he whom proud beauties of society vied with each other to win? He could not guess. A stray breeze laden with violet and hyacinth perfume stole in at the open window, ruffling the soft waves of auburn hair which shaded her alabaster forehead." It seems to me I have read something similar before, but it is good, anyhow. "Harold could not endure this placid, unruffled calm. His own veins were full of molten lava. With a wild and passionate cry he--"

Enter cook bearing a large, dripping piece of corned beef.

Cook. Please, Miss Anastasy, is dis de kin' of a piece ye done wanted? I thought I'd save ye de trouble o' comin' down.

Mrs. A. (desperately). It is!

[Exit cook, staring wildly.

Mrs. A. (resuming). "With a wild, passionate cry, he--"

Re-enter cook.

Cook. Ten cents for de boy what put in de wood, please, ma'am!

[Mrs. A. gives money; exit cook. Mrs. A., sighing, takes up MS. Clock strikes twelve; soon after the lunch-bell rings.]

Voice of Girl of Ten, calling: Mamma, why don't you come to lunch?

SCENE III. DINING-ROOM.

Enter Mrs. A.

Girl of Ten. Oh, what a mean lunch! Nothing but bread and ham. I hate bread and ham! All the girls have jelly-cake. Why don't we have jelly-cake? We used to have jelly-cake.

Mrs. A. You can have some pennies to buy ginger-snaps.

Girl of Ten. I hate ginger-snaps! When are you going to make jelly-cake?

Mrs. A. (sternly). When my book is done.

Girl of Ten (with inexpressible meaning): Hm!

Curtain falls.

SCENE IV. STUDY.

Enter Mrs. A. Children, still asleep; girls at school; deck again cleared for action.

Mrs. A. It is one o'clock. If I can be let alone until three I can finish that last chapter.

[Takes up pen; lays it down; reads a poem of Mrs. Browning to take the taste of ham-sandwiches out of her mouth, then resumes pen, and writes with increasing interest for fifteen minutes. Everything is steeped in quiet. Suddenly a faint murmur of voices is heard; it increases, it approaches, mingled with the tread of many feet, and a rumbling as of mighty chariot-wheels. It is only Barnum's steam orchestrion, Barnum's steam chimes, and Barnum's steam calliope, followed by an array of ruff-scruff. They stop exactly opposite the house. The orchestrion blares, the chimes ring a knell to peace and harmony, the calliope shrieks to heaven. The infants wake and shriek likewise. Exit Mrs. A. Curtain falls.]

SCENE V. STUDY.

Enter Mrs. A. Peace restored; children happy with nurse. Seizes pen and writes rapidly. Doorbell rings, cook announces caller; nobody Mrs. A. wants to see, but somebody she MUST see. Exit Mrs. A. in a state of rigid despair.

SCENE VI. HALL.

[Visitor gone; Mrs. A. starts for study. Enter Girl of Eight followed by Girl of Ten.]

Duettino.

Girl of Ten. Mamma, please give me my music lesson now, so I can go and skate; and then won't you please make some jelly-cake? And see, my dress is torn, and my slate-frame needs covering.

Girl of Eight. Where are my roller-skates? Where is the strap? Can I have a pickle? Please give me a cent. A girl said her mother wouldn't let her wear darned stockings to school. I'm ashamed of my stockings. You might let me wear my new ones.

[Mrs. A. gives music lesson; mends dress; covers slate-frame; makes jelly-cake and a pudding; goes to nursery and sends nurse down to finish ironing.]

SCENE VII. NURSERY.

[Mrs. A. with babies on her lap. Enter husband and father with hands full of papers and general air of having finished his day's work.]

Mr. A. Well, how is everything? Children all right, I see. You must have had a nice, quiet day. Written much?

Mrs. A. (faintly). Not very much.

Mr. A. (complacently). Oh, well, you can't force these things. It will be all right in time.

Mrs. A. (in a burst of repressed feeling). We need the money so much, Charles!

Mr. A. (with an air of offended dignity). Oh, bother! You are not expected to support the family.

[Mrs. A., thinking of that dentist's bill, that shoe bill, and the summer outfit for a family of six, says nothing. Exit Mr. A., who re-enters a moment later.]

Mr. A. You--a--haven't fixed my coat, I see.

Mrs. A. (with a guilty start). I--I forgot it!

Gibbering Fiend Conscience. Ha, ha! Ho, ho!

Curtain falls amid chorus of exulting demons.

* * * * *

I have reserved for the close numerous instances of woman's facility at badinage and repartee. It is there, after all, that she shines perennial and pre-eminent. You will excuse me if I give them to you one after another without comment, like a closing display of fireworks.

And first let me quote from Mrs. Rollins, as an instance of the way in which women often react upon each other in repartee, a little conversation which it was once her privilege to overhear:

"Margaret. I wonder you never have been married, Kate. Of course you've had lots of chances. Won't you tell us how many?

"Kate. No, indeed! I could not so cruelly betray my rejected lovers.

"Helen. Of course you wouldn't tell us exactly; but would you mind giving it to us in round numbers?

"Kate. Certainly not; the roundest number of all exactly expresses the chances I have had.

"Charlotte (with a sigh). Now I know what people mean by Kate's circle of admirers!"

* * * * *

A lady was discussing the relative merits and demerits of the two sexes with a gentleman of her acquaintance. After much badinage on one side and the other, he said: "Well, you never yet heard of casting seven devils out of a man." "No," was the quick retort, "they've got 'em yet!"

* * * * *

"What would you do in time of war if you had the suffrage?" said Horace Greeley to Mrs. Stanton.

"Just what you have done, Mr. Greeley," replied the ready lady; "stay at home and urge others to go and fight!"

* * * * *

It was Margaret Fuller who worsted Mrs. Greeley in a verbal encounter. The latter had a decided aversion to kid gloves, and on meeting Margaret shrank from her extended hand with a shudder, saying: "Ugh! Skin of a beast! skin of a beast!"

"Why," said Miss Fuller, in surprise, "what do you wear?"

"Silk," said Mrs. Greeley, stretching out her palm with satisfaction.

Miss Fuller just touched it, saying, with a disgusted expression, "Ugh! entrails of a worm! entrails of a worm!"

* * * * *

Mademoiselle de Mars, the former favorite of the Theatre de Francis, had in some way offended the Gardes du Corps. So one night they came in full force to the theatre and tried to hiss her down.

The actress, unabashed, came to the front of the stage, and alluding to the fact that the Gardes du Corps never went to war, said: "What has Mars to do with the Gardes du Corps?"

* * * * *

Madame Louis de Seur is daughter of the late Casimir Pier, who was Minister of the Interior during Thiers's administration. When once out of office, but still an influential member of the House, he once tried to form a new Moderate Republican party, meeting with but little success.

Once his daughter, who was sitting in the gallery, saw him entering the House all alone.

"Here comes my father with his party," she said.

* * * * *

I was greatly amused at the quiet reprimand given by a literary lady of New York to a stranger at her receptions, who, with hands crossed complacently under his coat-tails, was critically examining the various treasures in her room, humming obtrusively as he passed along.

The hostess paused near him, surveyed him critically, and then inquired, in a gentle tone: "Do you play also?"

* * * * *

A young girl being asked why she had not been more frequently to Lenten services, excused herself in this fashion, severe, but truthful: "Oh, Dr. ---- is on such intimate terms with the Almighty that I felt de trop."

* * * * *

At a reception in Washington this spring an admirable answer was given by a level-headed woman--we are all proud of Miss Cleveland--to a fine-looking army officer, who has been doing guard duty in that magnificent city for the past seventeen years. "Pray," said he, "what do ladies find to think about besides dress and parties?"

"They can think of the heroic deeds of our modern army officers," was her smiling reply.

* * * * *

Do you remember Lydia Maria Child's reply to her husband when he wished he was as rich as Croesus: "At any rate, you are King of Lydia;" and Lucretia Mott's humorous comment when she entered a room where her husband and his brother Richard were sitting, both of them remarkable for their taciturnity and reticence: "I thought you must both be here--it was so still!"

* * * * *

In my own home I recall a sensible old maid of Scotch descent with her cosey cottage and the dear old-fashioned garden where she loved to work. Our physician, a man of infinite humor, who honestly admired her sterling worth, and was attracted by her individuality, leaned over her fence one bright spring morning, with the direct question: "Miss Sharp, why did you never get married?"

She looked up from her weeding, rested on her hoe-handle, and looking steadily at his hair, which was of a sandy hue, answered: "I'll tell you all about it, Doctor. I made up my mind, when I was a girl, that, come what would, I would never marry a red-headed man, and none but men with red hair have ever offered themselves."

* * * * *

We all know women whose capacity for monologue exhausts all around them. So that the remark will be appreciated of a lady to whom I said, alluding to such a talker: "Have you seen Mrs. ---- lately?"

"No, I really had to give up her acquaintance in despair, for I had been trying two years to tell her something in particular."

A lady once told me she could always know when she had taken too much wine at dinner--her husband's jokes began to seem funny!

* * * * *

Lastly and--finally, there is a reason for our apparent lack of humor, which it may seem ungracious to mention. Women do not find it politic to cultivate or express their wit. No man likes to have his story capped by a better and fresher from a lady's lips. What woman does not risk being called sarcastic and hateful if she throws back the merry dart, or indulges in a little sharp-shooting? No, no, it's dangerous--if not fatal.

"Though you're bright, and though you're pretty, They'll not love you if you're witty."

Madame de Stae and Madame Reamier are good illustrations of this point. The former, by her fearless expressions of wit, exposed herself to the detestation of the majority of mankind. "She has shafts," said Napoleon, "which would hit a man if he were seated on a rainbow."

But the sweetly fawning, almost servile adulation of the listening beauty brought her a corresponding throng of admirers. It sometimes seems that what is pronounced wit, if uttered by a distinguished man, would be considered commonplace if expressed by a woman.

Parker's illustration of Choate's rare humor never struck me as felicitous. "Thus, a friend meeting him one ten-degrees-below-zero morning in the winter, said: 'How cold it is, Mr. Choate.' 'Well, it is not absolutely tropical,' he replied, with a most mirthful emphasis."

And do you recollect the only time that Wordsworth was really witty? He told the story himself at a dinner. "Gentlemen, I never was really witty but once in my life." Of course there was a general call for the bright but solitary instance. And the contemplative bard continued: "Well, gentlemen, I was standing at the door of my cottage on Rydal Mount, one fine summer morning, and a laborer said to me: 'Sir, have you seen my wife go by this way?' And I replied: 'My good man, I did not know until this moment that you had a wife!'"

He paused; the company waited for the promised witticism, but discovering that he had finished, burst into a long and hearty roar, which the old gentleman accepted complacently as a tribute to his brilliancy.

The wit of women is like the airy froth of champagne, or the witching iridescence of the soap-bubble, blown for a moment's sport. The sparkle, the life, the fascinating foam, the gay tints vanish with the occasion, because there is no listening Boswell with unfailing memory and capacious note-book to preserve them.

Then, unlike men, women do not write out their impromptus beforehand and carefully hoard them for the publisher--and posterity!

* * * * *

And now, dear friends, a cordial au revoir.

My heartiest thanks to the women who have so generously allowed me to ransack their treasuries, filching here and there as I chose, always modestly declaiming against the existence of wit in what they had written.

To various publishers in New York and Boston, who have been most courteous and liberal, credit is given elsewhere.

Touched by the occasion, I "drop into" doggerel:

If you pronounce this book not funny, And wish you hadn't spent your money, There soon will be a general rumor That you're no judge of Wit or Humor.

###

www.ingramcontent.com/pod-product-compliance
Lightning Source LLC
Chambersburg PA
CBHW071045290526
45795CB00004B/1338